Remedial treatment of wood rot and insect attack in buildings

R W Berry

Building Research Establishment
Garston
Watford
WD2 7JR

BUILDING RESEARCH ESTABLISHMENT
Garston
Watford
WD2 7JR

© Crown copyright
First published 1994

BR 256
ISBN 0 85125 626 0

Applications to reproduce illustrations or extracts from the text of this
book should be made to the Publications Manager at the Building
Research Establishment

❏ Contents

❏ Features

❏ Tables

❏ Foreword

This book draws on nearly 70 years of research and accumulated experience in the performance of wood in buildings. A distinguished line of timber scientists, originally at the Forest Products Research Laboratory and subsequently at the Princes Risborough Laboratory of BRE, has contributed to our understanding of the mechanisms of timber deterioration. This has led to the development of correct specifications, good building practice and guidance on the proper use of coatings and wood preservatives which will ensure optimum service life for timber components.

Wood is not only a traditional construction material; it also has important economic and environmental features which will enhance its use in the future, provided timber resources can be sustained and properly managed. It is, though, important that buildings with timber components should be appropriately maintained, and this often requires the application of remedial treatments which, if incorrectly specified and applied, may themselves cause harm. This book will assist everyone to diagnose the cause of any problem correctly and then to specify a safe and effective treatment.

I have no doubt that *Remedial treatment of wood rot and insect attack in buildings* will become an essential reference to all concerned with the conservation and maintenance of timber in buildings.

R G Courtney
Chief Executive
BRE

❏ Author's note

Timber is a highly versatile building material. Because it is often built into structures intended for long life, it is necessary to know how it can best be maintained. It is important, then, to be able to assess any timber which has been attacked by fungi or insects and apply the necessary remedial measures, paying particular attention to timbers having a load-bearing role.

BRE has already published *Recognising wood rot and insect damage in buildings*, and this book, *Remedial treatment of wood rot and insect damage in buildings*, is its natural companion. It describes procedures for inspecting buildings for damage by fungal growths and wood-boring insects, and the methods and materials for treating damaged timber. It is concerned only with problems generally found in the United Kingdom; other countries and parts of the world will often experience different conditions and forms of attack on wood (eg, termites in tropical regions). Particular attention is given to the health and safety aspects of treatment processes, with which the Health and Safety Executive have given considerable help.

Although timber is a versatile material — light, strong and readily cut to shape with simple tools — it does suffer the disadvantage that it can deteriorate when exposed to dampness. An important consideration, therefore, in the design of buildings has always been the protection of timbers from dampness. As a result, rapid deterioration of timbers in service is, today, exceptional rather than normal; however, when dampness does occur in a building, perhaps due to defective design or damage to the structure, timber deterioration can follow.

A thorough inspection of a building for attack by decay fungi, or by wood-boring insects, often results from the recommendations of a valuation survey at change of ownership, but may also follow the discovery of timber damage during refurbishment works. Whatever the origin for undertaking an inspection of the timber in a building, the purpose of this book is to advocate procedures to be taken by the professional timber surveyor and treatment contractor for inspection and remedial action. I hope, though, that the book will not only be of use to the timber surveyor and specialist treatment contractor, but also to others in the building industry with interests in this field: the general building surveyor, and the architect and the builder who believe in designing and building to exclude these problems.

(Wherever I use the word 'surveyor' in the text, I refer only to the professional timber surveyor and not necessarily to a fully qualified building surveyor.)

While the processes involved in treating timber in buildings are potentially hazardous and therefore should be assigned to specialist treatment contractors, it helps if building owners and users understand what is being done and why. For these reasons I have used technical terms only where standard words are not suitable, and where such terms are unavoidable, I have provided definitions in a glossary at the end of the book. In the first chapter I have also explained some very basic — some will say very obvious — facts about wood.

Reference is made in the text to UK legislation, particularly relating to health and safety issues. Readers should be aware that changes in legislation can occur and are becoming more common with the introduction of European Community Directives.

I could not have prepared this book without the help of many others, both at BRE and in other organisations. I am grateful to Eric Takens-Milne, a practising architect and writer, who has given considerable help in organising the material and drafting text. The Department of the Environment has given encouragement and, of course, the original funding for the research programmes from which the underlying knowledge and information contained in this book derive. The Health and Safety Executive and the British Wood Preserving and Damp-proofing Association have been generous with their help and suggestions for improvements. Also I thank the many BRE colleagues and former members of Timber Division and its precursors who have built up the body of knowledge on which I have been able to draw; and Peter Trotman, Head of BRE's Advisory Service, who has provided much useful advice on building and inspection matters.

Finally, in a technical work such as this, I do not presume to have described every situation or every problem that a surveyor or contractor might encounter, and how it may be handled. I shall welcome, then, receiving advice of errors or omissions and of suggestions for improvements in the contents of the book.

R W Berry

General principles of timber deterioration

Timber is one of the oldest construction materials known. It has been used since man created the first primitive dwellings and continues to be widely used by the construction industry. Its use as a building material is unlikely to diminish in the foreseeable future.

Timber used in construction: medieval (above) vs modern

However, it is susceptible to deterioration, particularly under damp conditions. As a first step towards understanding this deterioration and the remedies available, this chapter explains the nature of timber, and the agents and processes of deterioration.

Timber: the nature of the material

Wood, the substance of which timber is composed, consists of numerous microscopic cells, the principal components of which are cellulose and lignin. Laid down in the tree in layers as part of a seasonal cycle of growth, the cells produce the rings that appear in cross-section through stems and branches.

The older wood in the centre of the trunk is called the heartwood and is usually darker in colour than the outer part of the trunk, the sapwood. However, in some species such as spruce and beech, the visual distinction between heartwood and sapwood is not obvious. Moreover, identification of heartwood and sapwood of timber in service may be difficult when it is only partly exposed, perhaps covered by accumulated dust, and the only available light is artificial.

A section through the trunk of a tree showing growth rings, heartwood and sapwood

Sapwood of most timbers is markedly less durable than heartwood. The relative proportion of the two components varies significantly between species and the proportion of sapwood to heartwood is notably higher in smaller trees. This proportion also influences the effectiveness of preservative treatment since the sapwood of most timbers is more permeable to preservative fluids than is the heartwood. Large-section timbers found in many older buildings have a high ratio of heartwood to sapwood because they were cut from large trees with proportionately little sapwood. The smaller-section timbers used in modern construction tend to have a high proportion of sapwood.

Timber is broadly classified into two categories: hardwood and softwood. Hardwood timber is produced from broad-leaved deciduous trees (eg, oak, elm, mahogany and teak) while softwood is produced from coniferous trees (eg, pine, spruce and fir).

Hardwood timbers are not necessarily more durable than softwood timbers; the heartwood of some hardwood timbers is very durable (eg, in teak and oak), but the heartwood of others is rated as perishable (eg, in beech). Although older properties may contain principally hardwood structural timbers, buildings constructed since about 1800 normally contain softwood structural elements.

Strength and durability are essential properties required of timber in buildings, and in designing and maintaining buildings, the primary objective is to preserve the structural integrity by avoiding and rectifying deterioration. The main mechanisms of deterioration are:

A section through a trunk showing the varying proportions of sapwood and heartwood when small and large diameter logs are converted into timber beams

❏ decay by wood-rotting fungi

❏ infestation by wood-boring insects

THE LEVEL OF MOISTURE IN TIMBER AT WHICH FUNGAL DECAY STARTS

There is no precise moisture level at which fungi will attack timber since the moisture threshold for decay can vary slightly, depending on the timber type and the fungus species. Three important points need to be made, though, about the link between moisture content of timber and fungal decay.

❑ In practice, decay only occurs in damp timbers. In well designed and maintained buildings, timbers do not become damp.

❑ Although fungal decay in timber becomes possible only at a measured moisture content above about 22%, rapid decay is likely only at 26% and above.

❑ For practicable purposes, a timber surveyor or other person inspecting a building will normally assume that timber is only safe from fungal decay at a measured moisture content of 20% or below. This 2% difference provides a safety margin which allows for possible inaccuracies in moisture meter readings as well as for the inaccessibility of some parts of timbers such as built-in joist ends.

Decay by wood-rotting fungi

Mechanism of attack

Decay fungi, of which there are a number of commonly occurring species, are usually spread by microscopic, airborne spores. When these fungal spores settle on the surfaces of damp timber, they germinate and develop fine thread-like filaments called hyphae which penetrate the wood. Each hypha releases chemicals (enzymes) into the surrounding wood. Decay is caused by the process of these chemicals dissolving nutrients in the wood; the nutrients are then absorbed by the fungal hyphae, enabling further growth to take place. If the timber moisture content falls below about 22%, this mechanism can no longer operate and the decay process stops. Above about 22%, as growth extends through the wood, a fine network of threads is formed; this network is known as a mycelium. Mycelia of different fungi can vary in colour and appearance, helping in the identification process.

Behind the advancing front of the actively growing mycelium, the hyphae may fuse to form strands which conduct food and water. The

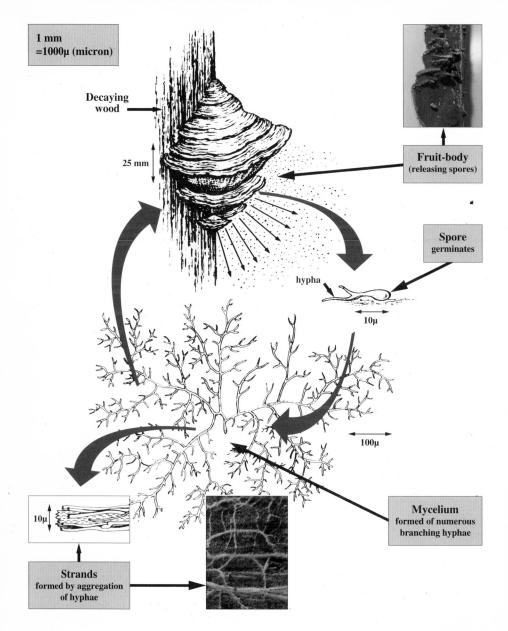

1 mm
=1000μ (micron)

Decaying wood

25 mm

Fruit-body
(releasing spores)

Spore germinates

hypha

10μ

100μ

Mycelium
formed of numerous
branching hyphae

10μ

Strands
formed by aggregation
of hyphae

The life cycle of a typical wood-rotting fungus

presence or absence of strands, their colour and size are all useful factors in identifying the specific types of fungi.

From time to time the fungal life cycle is completed when a spore-bearing fruit-body is produced on the surface of the decaying timber. This fruit-body will take a variety of shapes, sizes and colours which can also be used to identify the fungal species causing the decay.

Types of decay fungi

The correct identification of fungal growths found during an inspection is an important part of any remedial work. Some growths may be relatively harmless whilst others may indicate the need for particular remedial measures. Full descriptions of the characteristics needed to identify the type of fungus causing the decay are given in various publications. Among them is BRE's *Recognising wood rot and insect damage in buildings*[1].

There are a number of fungi which cause decay in building timbers. These are classified as either of the 'wet rot' type or as 'dry rot'.

Wet rot

As a general term, wet rot is used to cover the vast majority of fungal species responsible for timber decay. As mentioned earlier, wood is composed of cellulose and lignin. The wet rot fungi which can only attack the cellulose but not the lignin are called 'brown rots'; these wet rots leave the wood cross-cracked in cube-like shapes and brown in colour. Those which attack both cellulose and lignin are called 'white rots'; white rots leave the affected wood fibrous and pale in colour.

Typical brown rot damage (above) and white rot damage to timber

Dry rot

Serpula lacrymans, the only so-called dry rot fungus, is a particular species of brown rot. Affected wood is brown and shows cuboidal cracking; the 'cubes' are usually 25 mm^2 or more in size and tend to be larger than those of other brown rots. Although called dry rot, *S. lacrymans*, in common with all the wet rot types, requires the same minimum moisture content of about 22% for decay to progress.

Particular features of the dry rot fungus call for special consideration when specifying remedial work. Dry rot has a higher tolerance of alkaline conditions than the wet rots which allows it to spread through porous masonry materials in older properties. Wet rot fungi, although able to grow over the surface of non-wood materials, rarely grow through masonry materials.

The 'cube' size of dry rot (top) is usually larger than that for a wet rot (bottom, Coniophora puteana), although this cannot always be relied upon for distinguishing between the two types of rot

The dry rot mycelium and strands are often found growing at the interface between brickwork and lime-sand plaster. They may also be found in the mortar joints. This growth can only take place through relatively old lime mortars and lime plasters where the alkalinity has become reduced over time. High alkalinity, as found in fresh lime or cement mortar, will normally prevent growth through mortar joints, although growth over the surface of new brickwork is still possible. Fruit-bodies frequently appear on infected masonry surfaces, often in positions apparently remote from decaying timber.

The fungus derives no nutrition from masonry and causes no significant damage to the infected masonry itself, but the fungus is able to spread relatively rapidly from an initial outbreak through damp masonry to other damp timbers in contact with the infected wall. (Growth rates equivalent to almost 1 m per year have been recorded in buildings, and, with time, the fungus can spread several metres through masonry.) For this reason prompt remedial action is required after the discovery of dry rot.

Dry rot growth through masonry can only be sustained if both a timber food source and dampness are present. Removal of all timber from contact with an infected damp wall, and drying of the wall and associated timber, will therefore prevent further spread of and damage by the fungus. However, during drying of infected walls fruit-bodies may appear. It is also important to appreciate that the fungus

Typical dry rot outbreak

may lie dormant in dry timbers, including small fragments within dry walls, for up to a year and possibly longer in cooler areas such as cellars; and that if damp conditions are allowed to return the fungus may become active again.

Although the strands of the dry rot fungus can conduct moisture and nutrients to support growth, this ability is dependent on the moisture conditions in the surrounding wood or masonry. The fungus cannot colonise dry, well ventilated wood or masonry. However, the ability to conduct moisture does allow the fungus to spread from an attack in damp timber into adjacent, poorly ventilated voids where it is able to introduce additional water to marginally damp timber which might otherwise remain just below the moisture threshold for decay. Furthermore, gloss paints and other impervious coatings can trap moisture in masonry or stud walls. This will then allow the fungus to introduce sufficient moisture for the fungal mycelium to spread progressively through the coated masonry or timber. By this process the fungus can spread through voids such as those beneath poorly ventilated ground floors or behind painted internal panelling.

REUSE OF MASONRY FROM DRY ROT INFECTED SITES

Old bricks are often reused as facings in new buildings to achieve an old appearance. It is possible that some of these bricks may originate from dry rot infected buildings and therefore be contaminated with mycelium of the fungus. However, cases of infection of new buildings as a result of contamination by this means have never been recorded. This is almost certainly due to a number of factors which work against survival of the fungus.

❑ Any fungus surviving in or on the bricks will have very limited food resources for regrowth, provided that all wood fragments (fixing dowels, etc) have been removed. It is therefore unlikely that the fungus could grow onto, and subsequently decay, any adjacent new timbers before the building dries out

❑ The alkalinity of new mortar will prevent regrowth of the fungus until well after the building has dried to a level which, in itself, will prevent fungal growth.

❑ Old bricks are often incorporated in the external leaf of cavity walls, a position in which the only timber components are door and window joinery, and cladding. Such items are almost invariably either preservative treated or of naturally durable timber and, in the case of window and door joinery, are isolated from brickwork by damp proof membranes (DPMs).

It follows that the reuse of old bricks (or stone) from dry rot infected buildings should not present a hazard. Fungicidal treatment of the bricks therefore cannot be justified.

Brick or stone rubble from demolished buildings is frequently used as hardcore beneath new concrete ground floors. A number of cases of dry rot in the skirtings and door frames of new buildings have arisen where rubble contaminated with timber infected with the fungus had been used. This happened despite the presence of a polythene DPM, the fungus being able to pass through small perforations in the membrane to reach timber components in the building.

To avoid this problem special care should be taken to exclude all timber from hardcore used beneath concrete ground floors. Similarly, when redeveloping the sites of old buildings where cellars or basements are to be backfilled, care should be taken to remove all contaminated timber before rebuilding commences.

Other forms of fungal attack

Wet rots and dry rot are not the only types of fungal deterioration found in timber. 'Blue stain' and 'soft rot' can also adversely affect building timbers. Blue stain results from the growth of certain fungi which give rise to a black-blue colour in the affected timber. In buildings, blue stain is sometimes found in painted window joinery or panelling in bathrooms or kitchens subjected to condensation. Soft rot is the term applied to a type of superficial decay common on external timbers in very damp conditions. Normally soft rot is associated with unpainted external timber such as poles and fencing, and is of little or no significance in the remedial treatment of internal building timbers. Although these fungi do not cause significant weakening of timber, they are indicative of conditions suitable for the more damaging wet rot and dry rot decay fungi.

Insect infestation

Mechanism of attack

Many insect species are able to use wood as a food source. In doing so they can cause serious damage to timber by tunnelling into standing trees, freshly felled logs or wet decaying timber. A very small number, all beetles, are able to attack timber in the more or less dry conditions found in buildings.

These beetles all have a similar life cycle, although there are variations in the length of each stage in the life cycle, the type of wood attacked, and the extent and type of damage caused. Eggs laid by adults on timber surfaces, or in cracks in the timber, hatch to release very small grubs (larvae) which bore into the wood, feeding on the cellulose, lignin and other wood components, and creating a disinctive network of tunnels. The larvae of most wood-boring insects fill the tunnels with excreted wood pellets known as bore dust or frass. The size, shape and cross-section of the tunnels, and, to a lesser extent, the characteristics of the bore dust, are useful in identifying the species of insects.

After a period of one or more years' feeding, the larvae undergo a metamorphosis within the timber, passing through a pupal stage before changing into the adult form. These adult beetles then emerge, leaving the familiar 'woodworm' exit holes in the surfaces of the timber. The beetles do not themselves cause further damage, but, after mating, females often re-infest with their eggs in timbers near to those from which they have emerged; they may also fly or crawl some distance in search of suitable timber on which to lay their eggs. Damp conditions generally encourage infestation by most insects, and, in particular, deathwatch beetle and common furniture beetle.

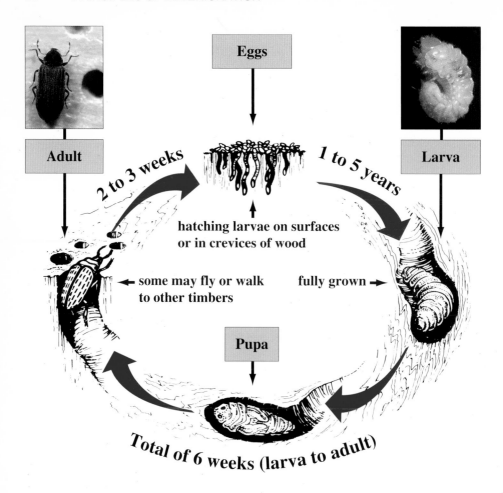

The life cycle of a typical wood-boring insect

Adult wood-boring insects are normally found only at certain times of the year and are rarely noticed — they usually die, anyway, within a few weeks of emerging from timber. A range of non-wood boring insects may be found, however, in buildings, and these other insects can be confused with the adults of wood-boring types; normally expert knowledge is needed to distinguish between them. Further information for identifying (and preventing misidentification of) wood-boring insects can be found in *Recognising wood rot and insect damage in buildings*.

The principle insects species attacking timber in buildings are:

Common furniture beetle *(Anobium punctatum)*

Commonly referred to as 'woodworm', this insect can attack the sapwood of all softwood and European hardwood timbers, such as oak and elm, in buildings throughout Britain.

In timbers where differentiation between heartwood and sapwood is not marked, such as in spruce, attack may spread across the entire cross-section of the timber. Although the insect is able to infest timbers with moisture contents typical of most well ventilated roofs and suspended ground floors, such infestations are usually only of moderate severity and low activity. **A severe active infestation indicates a dampness problem.** Infestations of internal joinery, staircases and mid-floors in buildings with central heating are unusual, and installation of such heating in existing buildings will tend to result in existing infestations dying out. Structural weakening is rare with this insect except in small-section timbers in particularly damp conditions; for example, in older dwellings with small-dimension joists cut from small trees with a high proportion of sapwood. However, floorboards may commonly require replacement where sapwood edges have been severely tunnelled.

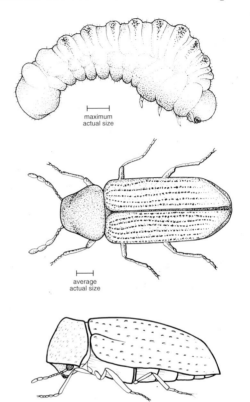

maximum
actual size

average
actual size

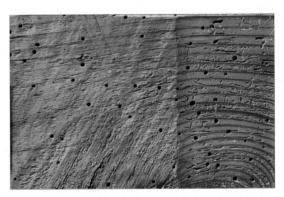

Common furniture beetle: larva, adult insect and the damage it causes

House longhorn beetle *(Hylotrupes bajulus)*

This insect is not common in the UK except in certain areas of north Surrey. It is principally found in roof timbers where it attacks the sapwood of exclusively softwood timbers, often resulting in structural weakening. The Building Regulations require that new roof timbers

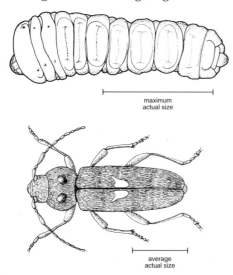

maximum
actual size

average
actual size

must be given suitable preservative pretreatment where they are to be used in designated local authority areas. The house longhorn beetle is not significantly encouraged by damp conditions.

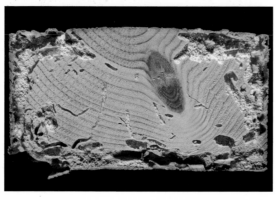

House longhorn beetle: larva, adult insect and the damage it causes

Deathwatch beetle *(Xestobium rufovillosum)*

Deathwatch beetle is common throughout the southern half of the United Kingdom; it is found less frequently in the north of England and is unknown in Scotland except for rare instances of 'imported' infested timbers.

Infestations are most common in large-dimension hardwood timbers such as oak and elm, although infestation may spread into adjacent softwood timbers; for example, infestations in hardwood wall plates commonly spread to softwood truss ends bearing on the plates. In exceptional cases, damage may be found in softwood timbers alone. Damp conditions as well as some fungal decay are necessary for establishment, and favour rapid development of an infestation. Damage is often localised around embedded joist ends or as cavities inside large-dimension beams which are subjected to damp conditions, extending into the heartwood of timbers where this has been affected by fungal decay.

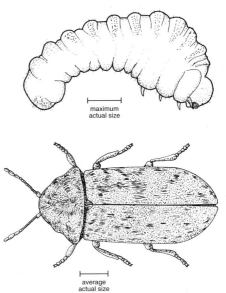

maximum
actual size

average
actual size

Deathwatch beetle: larva, adult insect and the damage it causes

Lyctus powderpost beetle *(Lyctus brunneus)*

Found worldwide, this insect derives its name from the severity of the damage it causes, often reducing the sapwood of susceptible species to a powdered mass within two to four years; heartwood is immune. Most tropical hardwood timbers are attacked as well as a limited number of coarse-pored European hardwood timbers such as oak, elm, ash and chestnut. Softwood timbers are immune, therefore most modern structural timbers are not affected. Hardwood timbers become less susceptible with age and can be regarded as immune after 10 to 15 years. In older properties with oak or elm beams, any powderpost beetle damage is almost certain to be extinct.

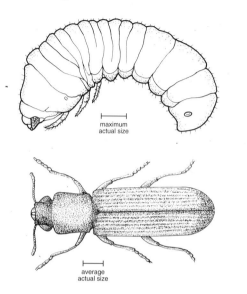

maximum
actual size

average
actual size

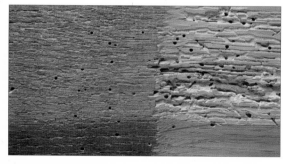

Lyctus powderpost beetle: larva, adult insect and the damage it causes

The start of infestation of timber components usually occurs prior to delivery to site, and usually continues in these timbers after installation in the building. Infestation is common in plywoods manufactured from susceptible timbers.

In addition a number of other wood-boring beetles (of which wood-boring weevils and the Ptilinus beetle are worth mentioning — see next page) may be encountered in buildings but are of less significance.

Wood-boring weevils *(Pentarthrum huttoni* and *Euophryum confine)*

Wood-boring weevils attack only damp, fungally decayed timber. Although they may increase the rate of deterioration by their tunnelling, they are not a primary cause of timber deterioration. Damp joist ends and the backs of skirting boards on damp walls are commonly attacked. No specific remedial treatment is necessary since infestations die out rapidly with drying of the affected timber.

Ptilinus beetle *(Ptilinus pectinicornis)*

This insect is rarely encountered in building timbers, being restricted to certain hardwoods such as beech or elm. Remedial treatment follows the same procedure described for common furniture beetle.

2 Outlines for remedial strategies

This chapter describes the basic strategies which are necessary for effective remedial treatment of fungal decay and insect attack. More detailed guidance is given in the chapters dedicated to each specific remedial function: Chapters 3, 4 and 5 for inspection, Chapter 6 for the remedial treatment of fungal decay and Chapter 7 for the remedial treatment of insect attack.

In all cases the remedial strategy must consist of two stages. First, inspection of the building and second, remedial work. The primary objectives of inspection are to:

❑ identify building defects causing dampness

❑ determine whether there is fungal or insect attack in the building and to what extent timbers have deteriorated

❑ decide on appropriate remedial work

In many cases, especially with fungal decay, the remedial work will need to concentrate on repairs to eliminate specific moisture sources, repair or replacement of damaged timbers, and improvements to reduce levels of dampness in the building. In other cases, the additional use of wood preservatives may be appropriate. Naturally, there will be cases where combinations of these remedial measures are involved.

Failure by a timber surveyor to properly identify the cause and full extent of the fungal decay or insect attack, and to specify appropriate treatment, can lead to further spread of decay or infestation; this in turn can have serious financial consequences for the building owner or a subsequent purchaser, and possible legal implications for the surveyor concerned (and his employer).

Remedial strategy for fungal decay

Fungal decay of timber can only start and progress when the timber becomes damp; in other words, its moisture content rises above about 22%. Therefore, in inspection and remedial treatment, the location and removal of the causes of dampness must be paramount. This point cannot be over emphasised.

In a building, the moisture content of different timbers will vary with the time of year and with levels of heating and ventilation. However, in a properly designed, well built, well maintained property, the moisture content of internal timbers is unlikely to exceed 20% for any significant period of time. Timber should remain well below 20% throughout its service life, except for occasional and transient superficial wetting; for example, as a result of condensation in unheated voids such as those beneath ground floors.

If the level of moisture in timbers rises above the threshold for decay for significant periods, then, logically, some failure in design, construction or maintenance has occurred which allows this excessive moisture into the building. Locating and remedying the

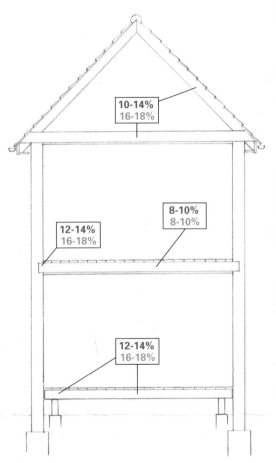

The typical moisture content of the timber components of a house in summer (red) and winter (blue)

failure are the first steps in dealing with fungal decay. Only when these have been achieved should repair, replacement and treatment of affected timbers be considered.

Step 1: locating sources of dampness

The ability to identify building defects requires training and experience, and a methodical approach to inspection and recording. All failures in design, construction and maintenance which could result in water entering the building should be carefully noted. (See Chapters 4 and 5 for procedures for undertaking inspections and for checklists for the parts of a building that should be investigated.)

Step 2: repairing defects

The parts of the building which have failed, leading to the ingress of water, must be repaired. Typical defects which give rise to water entry, dampness and consequent decay — and therefore require immediate repair — are failure of rainwater goods and roof coverings, defective rendering, inadequate ventilation of roofs and suspended timber floors, defective damp proof courses, and plumbing leaks.

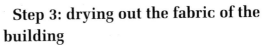

Step 3: drying out the fabric of the building

After locating and removing the causes of water entry, excess moisture must be removed from the fabric by drying. In its simplest form, this will be no more than temporary increases in the ventilation of the affected area. In some situations, it may be necessary to introduce, temporarily, substantially increased levels of heating and natural or mechanical ventilation (eg, by dehumidifiers or industrial forced-air heaters).

Step 4: identifying and repairing or replacing decayed timbers

Decayed timbers will usually be found associated with the sources of dampness located in Step 1. The full extent of deterioration of timbers must be determined and those which are unacceptably weakened be repaired or replaced, either with preservative pretreated timbers or substitute units in steel or concrete.

Step 5: identifying and protecting sound timbers at risk during drying

In lightweight constructions or those with only minor localised dampness, timbers can be expected to dry rapidly. Where heavier masonry construction and severe wetting are encountered, timbers in contact with damp masonry may remain above the threshold of moisture content for decay for several weeks or months. In these cases, the temporary protection of timber by in situ application of wood preservative is often needed.
Where drying cannot be achieved within a reasonable time, or where there is a real risk of future wetting, physical isolation of all timbers from persistently damp masonry, or replacement with either non-wood substitutes or preservative pretreated timber, is necessary.

Special measures for dry rot

The broad principles for dealing with fungal decay apply equally to wet rots and dry rot. Correct diagnosis of dry rot is essential because this fungus can spread rapidly through damp masonry and is less likely to be localised around an immediate source of moisture. Hence, care is needed in establishing the full extent of a dry rot outbreak as it may have spread extensively behind plaster, dry linings or panelling. The potential for growth of the fungus from infected masonry onto damp timbers also requires a more rigorous approach to the drying out of timbers and their isolation from infected masonry.

Remedial strategy for insect attack

Although damp conditions encourage infestation by some insects such as deathwatch beetle or common furniture beetle, infestation may start and continue in the absence of any specific dampness problem. Assessment for insect attack does not therefore call for a general inspection of the overall state of repair or maintenance of a building, although such information is clearly of value as an indicator of timbers most at risk.

The fundamental principles in dealing with insect infestation (described in the following steps) are the location of damaged timbers, correct identification of the causal insect and the specification of the appropriate remedial measures.

Step 1: locating timbers showing evidence of attack

The location of insect attack can only be achieved by direct visual inspection of all timbers for evidence of insect exit holes. Particular attention should be paid to areas affected by general long term dampness.

Step 2: identifying the type of damage

Correct identification of the insect causing damage is important, not only in deciding the appropriate form of timber treatment but also in deciding if any action is required at all. Insect species causing damage in standing trees or freshly felled logs all leave evidence of tunnels in the timber but require no remedial action. Also some insects are only active in damp, decayed timber and require only those measures that are necessary to deal with the associated fungal decay. Identification relies largely on the size and shape of the insect tunnels and exit holes, together with the timber species being attacked.

Step 3: assessing activity and extent of damage

Freshly cut exit holes and recently ejected bore dust are the most commonly available indicators of insect activity, although dust may be also shaken from timbers subjected to foot traffic (eg, on stairs). Insect larvae extracted by probing of the tunnelled timber are a more certain guide but in practice are usually difficult to find.

Probing timbers with a pointed instrument or drilling can be used where necessary to determine the depth to which timbers have been severely damaged by tunnelling.

Step 4: treating active infestations

Treatment of infestations identified as active almost always consists of applying an insecticidal wood preservative to the surfaces of the timbers; this is usually done by spraying or, with deeper seated infestations, by drilling and injection. Severely weakened timbers should be repaired or replaced with preservative pretreated timbers, or steel or concrete substitute units.

Where there is doubt as to whether an insect infestation is active or extinct, remedial treatment may be specified to provide a guarantee of freedom from infestation. However, in these circumstances, the decision to treat should only be taken after a COSHH (Control of Substances Hazardous to Health Regulations 1988) assessment has been made in which other factors such as ease of access for future treatment are considered. (See Table 7.1.)

The purpose of the assessment is to identify the need for the use of hazardous substances (such as wood preservatives), to determine the level of risk associated with the particular use, and to identify appropriate measures to protect operatives and others. The significance of a COSHH assessment is explained more fully in Chapter 8.

3 Preparation for building inspection

In most cases of building inspection, it is unlikely that the timber surveyor will be asked to examine premises for fungal decay or insect infestation alone. While examining timbers for one type of damage (eg, fungal decay), it makes sense to check for the existence of the other (insect attack). This chapter alerts the surveyor to the need to agree with the client how he, the surveyor, is to undertake the work; it describes the tools normally used for inspection (for both fungal decay and insect infestation), and it also deals with recording the findings of the inspection, and how matters concerned with the structural integrity and safety of the building should be approached.

Agreeing the scope of inspection

The timber surveyor must establish with the client the extent of the inspection required. This should preferably be part of a written contract, including any works necessary to gain access to subfloor timbers and roof spaces. The surveyor will need to agree with the client the amount of access required. In some cases this will require the client or the surveyor to remove floor coverings and lift floorboards.

Although, on occasion, inspection of only part of a building may be appropriate or indeed be requested by a client, it is not generally an advisable approach. In a case of fungal decay, for example, failure to identify and remedy all moisture sources can lead to delay in drying the building and, consequently, to further decay. Where a surveyor cannot avoid a partial inspection, the extent of the inspection and the possible consequences of the limitations imposed must be made clear in the inspection report. Failure to do this could result in a financial liability to the surveyor or his employer for any subsequent deterioration of the property. Such liability may occur even where no charge was made for an inspection.

Timber surveyors may or may not be professionally qualified to give opinions on structural matters and this must be made clear to the client. There is, though, a legal duty on the part of the surveyor, however qualified, to alert a client to any building defects which he recognises and which he judges could endanger the structure or its occupants (eg, dangerous electrical wiring or a leaking flue).

Inspection equipment

The following list is representative of the equipment which the typical professional timber surveyor may have to hand on site:

❑ notebook, pens, pencils

❑ bolster or wrecking bar to lift floorboards; claw hammer and nails to refix them

❑ knife, bradawl or sharp screwdriver to probe for softening and 'brash' splintering

❑ hammer to 'sound' large-dimension timbers and detect internal decay or cavities (perhaps the previously-mentioned claw hammer used to refix floorboards)

❑ hand lens giving a × 10 magnification

❑ moisture meter (see page 25)

❑ surveyor's mirror (effectively a mirror on the end of a stick — see page 26) and, possibly, borescope (a type of optical probe — see page 27) to examine voids with limited access

❑ rotary power and hand drills, and standard and masonry drill bits; ratchet and joist braces, and wood-boring bits and augers to assess damage within large-dimension timbers and to drill holes for the borescope if used

❑ camera to record conditions and defects or failures; spare films and batteries

❑ robust torch with a strong beam

❑ small paint brush, forceps and containers to collect specimens; labels for identifying the contents of containers

❑ binoculars to aid external inspection

❑ compass to establish orientation of the building

❏ ladder (3 m, collapsible)

❏ protective helmet, overalls and gloves

❏ filter mask (if required to inspect a dusty area or roof void containing, for example, glass fibre insulation)

Some of the equipment used for inspecting buildings for fungal and insect attack

From this list of equipment the essential tools are the moisture meter suitable for use on timber, the probe (such as a bradawl) for detecting decay-softening and insect damage of timbers, a sounding hammer, a bolster or wrecking bar, a powerful torch, and some means of examining spaces which are awkward to reach such as subfloor voids and where only limited opening up is possible. For this last item a simple surveyor's mirror will suffice in most situations, although a more sophisticated optical probe such as a borescope does allow inspection of voids through drilled holes with a diameter as small as 10 mm.

Moisture meter

Using a moisture meter
A moisture meter is an essential instrument for detecting the less obvious sources of dampness and, therefore, possible incidence of fungal decay. Two types are available: the most commonly used measures the electrical conductivity between two probes pushed into the timber. The wetter the wood the higher the conductivity. The main limitation of this type is that contamination of the timber with any inorganic salts (including those

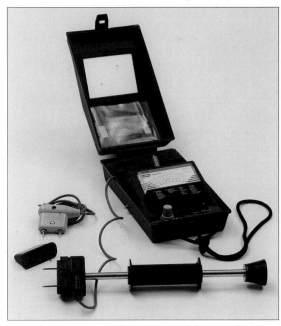

A conductivity-type moisture meter with a standard probe (left) and a hammer probe (below)

contained in some types of preservative) will give a misleadingly high reading; also the short probes normally supplied can result in surface moisture being identified as a deeper seated dampness problem, or in failing to reach and detect dampness in large timbers. These latter limitations can be overcome by the use of longer, insulated, hammer probes (see photograph on this page).

An alternative type based on the capacitance of timber is also available. This has the advantage that probes do not have to be inserted into the wood. However, whilst apparently not affected by salt contamination, this type may also result in confusion in discriminating between surface and deeper seated moisture.

Using a conductivity-type moisture meter

Plotting 'moisture maps' to identify dampness areas
Moisture meter readings,
taken at about 1 m
spacings, of floorboards
and exposed joists, wall
plates and lintels,
entered into sketches of
plans and elevations of
the building — each floor
in turn — provide a good
guide to areas of dampness
where decay is most likely
to be present. Such maps can
also help to indicate the
location of any moisture
source. Mapping of moisture
readings from masonry
surfaces can also provide a
useful guide to moisture
sources. Particular care is
needed, though, in interpreting
such readings as they can be
misleading due to contamination
with salts; this is a common problem in walls suffering from rising
damp.

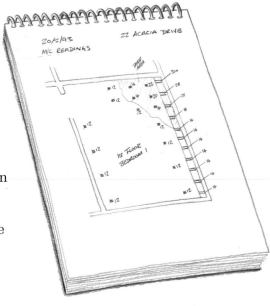

Moisture meter readings incorporated into a plan sketch

Surveyor's mirror

This is a mirror with a long or telescopic handle (a mirror-on-a-stick)
to allow inspection of areas which
are awkward to see. It is a simple
device which, used in
combination with a powerful
torch, helps in the
inspection of voids
without excessive
opening up.

Using a surveyor's mirror to inspect parts of timbers not in direct line of sight

Borescope

The borescope is a more advanced alternative to the surveyor's mirror, allowing inspection of hidden voids with only minimal drilling of holes.

It consists of three component parts (see photograph on this page):

❏ a light source, usually a mains-powered transformer

❏ a flexible light guide

❏ a rigid probe which has an eyepiece at one end connected by an optical system (passing through a steel tube of approximately 10 mm diameter) to a viewing lens at the other end

The borescope normally requires a hole to be made in the floor, wall or other building component through which the probe is inserted; the hole needs to be only slightly larger than the diameter of the probe, usually little more than 10 mm. The surveyor will therefore need to carry a drill and bits capable of cutting these holes as well as plugs or filler to close the holes. Most borescopes are limited to a probe length of about 300 mm which is adequate for the majority of inspections of underfloor voids or wall cavities. Illumination of the void under examination is provided by a light source feeding light to the tip of the probe by means of a flexible optical fibre light guide. Observations are made through the eye piece which is connected by the optical system to a small lens at the tip of the probe. Standard probes are fitted with lenses which provide a view at right angles to the probe. Flexible remote control types are available which enable inspection of some more inaccessible parts of buildings.

A borescope comprising the light source, flexible light guide and probe

A borescope can be used to inspect hidden parts of buildings with minimal disturbance

Considerable caution is needed in interpreting the view given by these devices as the light source will not normally illuminate an area more than about 500 mm from the probe. For this reason not all timber surveyors consider it worthwhile routinely including a borescope as a part of their equipment, particularly in view of the bulk of the transformer and the need for an electrical supply. A simpler, battery powered version of a borescope may be found to be a suitable alternative.

Sounding hammer

Decayed wood and rot cavities can often be detected by the change in note when timber is 'sounded' by striking it with a small hammer. The method is particularly useful for larger dimension timbers. Sounding should be undertaken sequentially around and over an area vulnerable to water penetration or suspected as being defective. There is no specific note associated with decayed wood; it is the change in note between unaffected and decay affected wood (usually a lower and duller tone) that provides a clue to the defect.

Recording of inspection findings

A comprehensive, planned approach should be adopted towards inspections to avoid the possibility that areas could be unintentionally missed. For this reason many professionals use a standardised checklist and report form. (BRE's *Surveyor's checklist for rehabilitation of traditional housing*[2] and the checklists in Chapters 4 and 5 form a useful basis for this kind of aid.)

Drawings of floor plans and elevations, incorporating the moisture maps already described, help plot the position and extent of deterioration

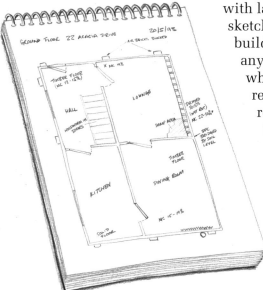

It is good practice, particularly with larger buildings, to draw a sketch plan of each floor of a building, marking on the plans any defects or deterioration which are observed, and recording those timbers which require replacement and those which require remedial preservative treatment. These plans can also incorporate the detailed moisture maps described in the section of this chapter on the moisture meter.

A photographic record of damaged timbers and features of (and defects in) design and construction can be invaluable; for instance, in showing the client the extent or severity of damage in areas awkward for access and in explaining recommendations for remedial work. (It can also provide a record in the event of a dispute regarding the competence of the survey.)

The age and history of the building, type of construction, any previous maintenance or repair work, and any previous preservative treatment of timbers are all items of information that the timber surveyor should ascertain, as far as is reasonably possible, before starting the inspection.

4 External inspection of buildings for sources of dampness

For the purpose of this book both this chapter and Chapter 5 are written on the basis that a full and comprehensive survey of timber condition is required. As noted in Chapter 3, partial surveys, although sometimes appropriate, are not generally advisable. The extent to which a timber surveyor is able to inspect the outside of a building will vary and depend on its height, whether there is scaffolding erected, whether access can be gained to roof surfaces, etc. However, the surveyor should make all possible efforts to view features which might allow the entry of water. A pair of low-power binoculars can often be used at ground level to view inaccessible high level features. He should particularly examine those timber components where end-grain is exposed to the weather or susceptible to wetting (eg, rafter ends).

Since penetration by rain is one of the chief causes of dampness, the checklists which follow in this chapter and the next have been constructed on the assumption that the surveyor will normally examine first the outside of the building. However, the order of inspection of a building is a matter for the professional surveyor to decide and may be influenced by other factors outside the scope of this book. The most important consideration is that the survey should be comprehensive and logical so as to avoid the possibility that defects are missed.

Pitched roofs and chimneys

Typical defects for identification by external inspection (with numbered references to the figure on this page and the next):

❑ paint or other protective coatings on barge (1), soffit and fascia boards (2) failing; rot in these components

❑ valley tiles (3) missing, damaged or defective

❑ gutters (4) which are missing, too small for catchment areas, blocked, broken, hung too low, or with back fall or inadequate fall to carry away all surface water

❑ overhanging of eaves and verges (5) insufficient to prevent wetting of walls below (particularly with walls facing prevailing winds and, consequently, driving rain) and penetration of water to internal surfaces

❑ ventilation gaps into roof spaces at eaves (6) missing, blocked or inadequate (also check internally)

Points in a typical pitched roof structure where dampness problems can occur

❑ underfelt not turned into gutter or sagging behind fascia board (7)

❑ roof–wall flashings, flashings to chimneys (8), dormer windows and other upstands and abutments missing, not adequately dressed into brick work or damaged; chimney cavity trays (9) absent or defective

❑ ridge tiles, roof tiles or slates (10) missing, damaged or defective

❑ valley gutters (11) blocked or damaged

❑ unused chimneys (12) badly capped (including not providing adequate ventilation to flues) or damaged; flaunching of chimney pots (13) poorly executed or damaged

❑ chimney stack (14) crumbling and mortar joints deteriorating; render cracking or detaching from chimney

❑ parapet gutters and outlets (15) blocked or damaged (parapet gutters are particularly prone to leakage and require careful examination)

Flat roofs

Typical defects for identification by external inspection (with numbered references to the figure on the next page):

❑ drainage channels (16) missing, blocked or leaking

❑ ventilation gaps or grilles or air bricks into roof spaces at eaves (17) missing, blocked or inadequate (also check internally, if possible)

❑ roof–wall flashings (18) missing or defective

❑ coping detail (19) not correct

❑ waterproof layers (20) damaged

❑ gutters (21) missing, too small for catchment areas, blocked, broken, hung too low, or with back fall or inadequate fall to carry away all surface water

❑ roof construction (22) not correct leading to ponding of water or sagging (ponding or sagging usually indicates dampness in the roof structure)

❑ overhanging of eaves (23) insufficient to prevent wetting of walls below (particularly with walls facing prevailing winds and, consequently, driving rain) and penetration of water to internal surfaces

❑ roof falls (24) not adequate

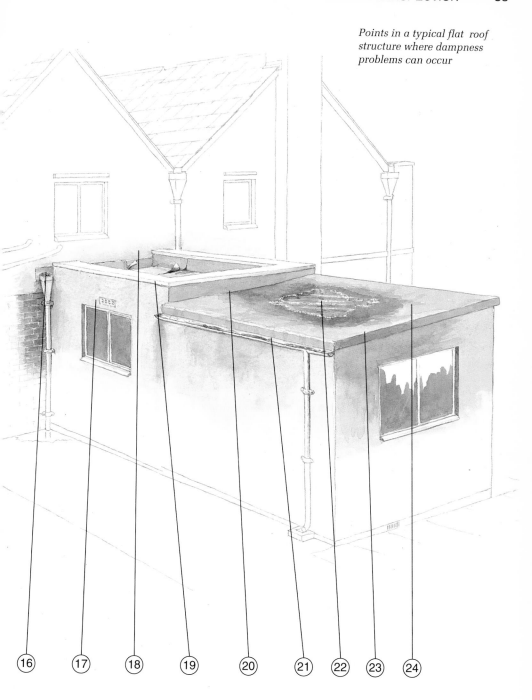

*Points in a typical flat roof
structure where dampness
problems can occur*

External walls

Typical defects for identification by external inspection (with numbered references to the figure on this page and the next):

❑ brickwork (25) cracking, spalling or crumbling (due to movement or sulphate attack); mortar joints deteriorating or badly repointed

Points in typical external walls where dampness problems can occur

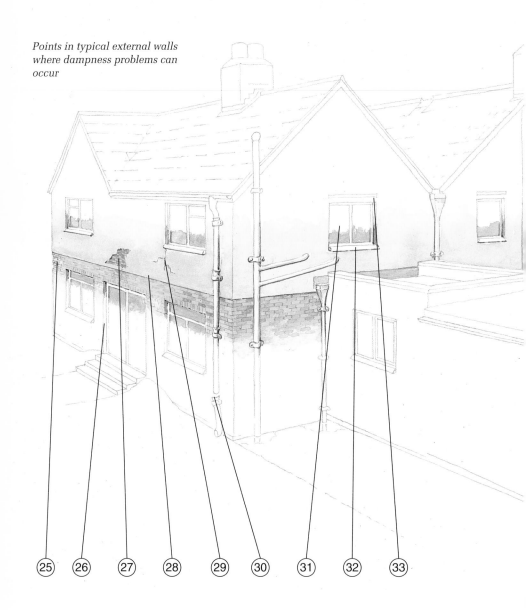

❏ vertical and horizontal DPCs to openings (26) (eg, window and door frames) and copings missing

❏ render (27) missing, cracking or detaching from brickwork; render with inadequate drip (28)

❏ other surface coatings (29) cracking or deteriorating

❏ hoppers and downpipes (30) which are too small or missing, blocked, corroded or broken, leading to leakage or overflows and wetting of walls (streaks of green algal growth on walls adjacent to or below rainwater goods indicate possible leaking; isolated damp patches and algal growths indicate other possible defects such as overflows from tanks splashing onto walls)

❏ wood doors and windows (31) poorly designed or positioned, including being set too far forward in the external leaf; wood doors, windows and lintels in solid walls; wood doors and windows with no protective coatings or with cracked or flaking finishes, and with cracked or missing putty; joinery adjacent or near to defective or poorly applied sealants; cills (32) without proper throating, fall or drips, or with blocked weep holes

❏ ledges (33) without falls or weathering to shed water

❏ projections (34) (eg, cornices and string courses) not capped

Joinery frames set into the external leaf of a building will almost inevitably remain damp for prolonged periods, even if well maintained. For this reason modern external joinery is usually preservative impregnated during manufacturing, unless constructed from naturally decay-resistant hardwood timbers such as oak.

Poorly designed, untreated softwood frames can decay within a period of a few years if installed in walls exposed to prevailing weather.

Ground level

Typical defects for identification by external inspection (with numbered references to the figure on this page and the next):

❑ damp proof courses (DPCs) bridged by secondary structures (35), raised soil levels (36) or external render or mortar (37)

❑ downpipes (38) discharging at the bases of walls

❑ external soil pipes (39) discharging at the bases of walls

Points in a typical structure at the wall–ground junction where dampness problems can occur

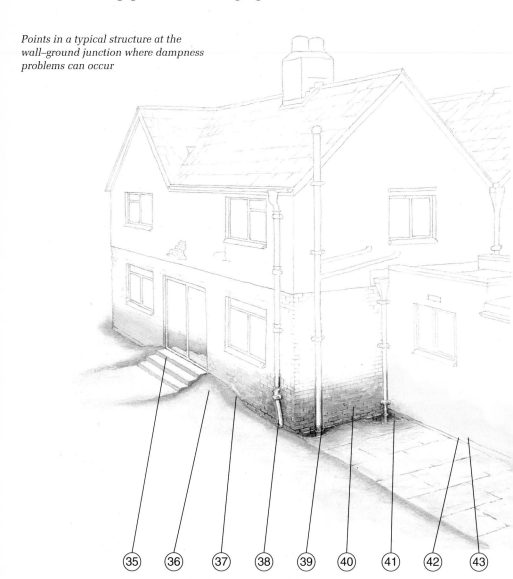

❏ DPCs (40) missing, bridged or damaged leading to rising damp (missing DPCs are generally a problem found in older buildings)

❏ impervious surfaces (41) alongside walls (eg, patios and driveways) not laid so that water flows away from the bases of the walls

❏ DPCs (42) too close to the external ground (particularly if the ground is an unyielding surface such as concrete) so that rainwater and overflow water splashes onto the brickwork above the DPCs

❏ DPCs and damp proof membranes (DPMs) (43) not properly lapped allowing ground water to rise up in the structure

❏ gullies and drains (44) missing, blocked, damaged or inadequate

With a suspended timber floor:

❏ air bricks (45) which are missing, blocked up or inadequate in size

❏ air bricks which are not sleeved through cavity walls and which have become blocked with rubble, mortar droppings, etc

❏ air bricks which are insufficient in number (ideally, for a given length of wall the free area of all the air bricks should average not less than 1500 mm²/m) or not evenly distributed. In older properties, one 230 × 230 mm traditional terracotta air brick for each 2 m run should be adequate

❏ air bricks which are only installed on one side or two adjacent sides of a building, so preventing or limiting the flow of air through the whole void

❏ the absence of a free air path (or of an adequate air path) between air bricks in opposing walls

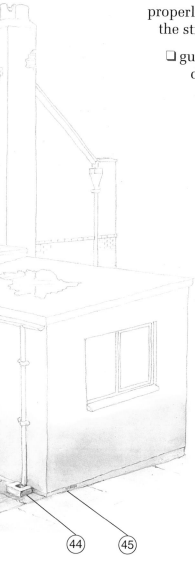

5 Internal inspection of buildings for dampness, decay and insect attack

Having completed an external examination of the property, the timber surveyor can then progress to an examination of the interior of the building for evidence of dampness and timber deterioration. Defects noted during the external inspection will need to be followed through to associated internal timbers and surfaces, and assessed for their significance.

In carrying out an inspection, a consistent, logical approach is needed. The importance in adopting a set procedure, for example starting in the roof space and working down, is to ensure that all areas are covered.

Detection of dampness

Although there may be no evidence of apparent water entry or dampness on exposed surfaces, externally or internally, in any part of the building, it should not be assumed by the surveyor that dampness problems do not exist in hidden parts of the structure; for example, beneath suspended ground floors or in embedded lintels or joist ends. In the absence of obvious symptoms of dampness, inspections should still include examination of the hidden parts on a sample basis: sufficient to disclose significant decay. All incidence of dampness in a building should be regarded as potential causes of decay, even where no decay can be detected at the time of inspection.

Typically, defects may be revealed by water staining, damp patches or fungal growths on timber, wallpaper or painted surfaces; evidence of severe insect attack may point to persistent, moderate dampness. External defects allowing water to enter are more likely to show during or immediately following heavy rain. Internal inspection at, or shortly after, heavy rain can help, therefore, in the identification of water penetration.

Careful internal investigation should be made in all cases where apparent defects are picked up during the external inspection, even though water or dampness may not be evident internally at the time of inspection.

As described in Chapter 3, timber moisture contents throughout the inspected area should be recorded using a moisture meter, paying particular attention to timbers in contact with masonry.

The following sections give guidance on inspection of particular areas for evidence of sources of dampness.

Roof spaces

Wherever possible, inspection of pitched roofs should reach to the limits of voids (although this is often very difficult), especially those less accessible parts where water leakage or penetration may remain unnoticed by building owners and occupiers. Particular areas for examination include:

❏ roof joists and tile battens below missing or damaged tiles, around defective chimney flashings and near deteriorating chimney brickwork

❏ wall plates beneath valley gutters, whether known to be leaking or not

❏ joists, wall plates and rafter ends where eaves ventilation is poor

❏ redundant chimneys with air bricks or grilles which are absent, blocked, defective or inadequate

Flat roofs are normally impossible to inspect internally without damage to roof coverings or linings. Only where there are grounds for suspecting defective design leading to internal condensation, or there is evidence of leakage or sagging of the decking, is opening up normally regarded as justified; inspection by borescope may provide a good guide to condition. Particular attention should be given to:

❏ joists and decking below damaged metal sheeting or waterproof membranes, and areas of sagging or ponding

❏ joists and decking with areas of high moisture content

❏ wall plates, joist ends and decking adjacent to defective roof–wall flashings

❏ joists, decking and lintels near poorly detailed copings

❏ flat roofs of 'cold deck' design

One problem that an external inspection cannot identify is that of dampness resulting from condensation in a roof space. This can exacerbate dampness arising from leakage and thus accelerate timber decay. In a pitched roof void, condensation always points to

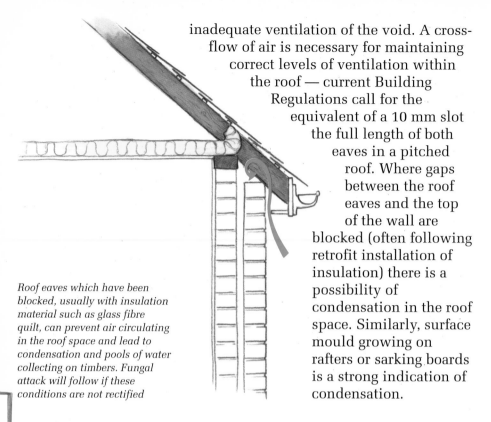

inadequate ventilation of the void. A cross-flow of air is necessary for maintaining correct levels of ventilation within the roof — current Building Regulations call for the equivalent of a 10 mm slot the full length of both eaves in a pitched roof. Where gaps between the roof eaves and the top of the wall are blocked (often following retrofit installation of insulation) there is a possibility of condensation in the roof space. Similarly, surface mould growing on rafters or sarking boards is a strong indication of condensation.

Roof eaves which have been blocked, usually with insulation material such as glass fibre quilt, can prevent air circulating in the roof space and lead to condensation and pools of water collecting on timbers. Fungal attack will follow if these conditions are not rectified

Living areas

The surveyor should examine and check all surfaces, horizontal and vertical, as he progresses through the building. If he finds evidence of dampness in timbers, joinery or masonry (either visually or by use of the moisture meter), he must establish the source. Elements for inspection should include:

❑ bearing ends of joists, lintels, wall plates, fixing blocks, bond timbers, and door and window frames in solid walls close to defective guttering or downpipes, deteriorating brickwork, or cracked or missing rendering

❑ timber adjacent to obvious areas of dampness caused by building defects such as building rubble and mortar droppings bridging wall cavities, and other defects causing wetting

❑ battens supporting dry linings to damp walls

❑ skirtings and timber wall panelling

❑ redundant chimneys with air bricks or grilles which are absent, blocked, defective or inadequate

Damp patches or stains on a chimney breast may indicate condensation in the flue due to a non-existent or defective lining and to lack of ventilation, although hygroscopic salts resulting from flue gases may also be a cause. In such cases, timber in contact with chimney brickwork should be examined for the signs and effects of dampness.

One phenomenon which is not always obvious but which can, nevertheless, affect timber in buildings is rain penetration of external walls; usually penetration, by driving rain, of walls facing the prevailing winds. External evidence of this is not always apparent, and may not necessarily be seen on internal walls. Timber joist ends and timber lintels embedded in exposed solid walls, or cavity walls where it is suspected that insulation material or mortar droppings have bridged the cavity, should always be checked for moisture content using a moisture meter. This will require some lifting of floorboards for access.

Timber ground floors

Wherever possible, suspended timber floors should be inspected by lifting sufficient floorboards to ascertain whether there is adequate provision for cross-ventilation (ie, air bricks). In particular the surveyor should check:

❑ the existence and effectiveness of ventilation openings in external and cross-walls

❑ that underfloor voids are not blocked with rubble

❑ that there is at least 75 cm vertical distance between the bottom of the joists and the ground, oversite or rubble

❑ that there are DPCs between bearing timbers and a sleeper wall beneath

Water staining, water droplets or mould on the underside of the timber floor are all strong indications (in the absence of other causes) of severe condensation resulting from inadequate ventilation.

Kitchens, bathrooms and understairs cupboards

Kitchens and bathrooms are susceptible to both leakage and condensation and should therefore be inspected for dampness; also cupboards and voids beneath stairs because these areas can remain unventilated for long periods. Sealant around basins baths, basins and sinks should be inspected for gaps and consequent water leakage.

Basement and cellar areas

Underground areas are particularly vulnerable to water penetration and poor ventilation, and, consequently, to fungal decay of any timber used in their construction; this includes timber used in basement ceilings and battens supporting dry linings in, for example, basements which have been converted or refurbished.

Unless a cellar or basement has been effectively waterproofed by tanking of the walls, acceptably dry conditions usually depend upon good ventilation. Areas where there is minimal or no provision for through ventilation should be given particular attention during a survey.

Plumbing and drainage in hidden areas

Corrosion and poor fitting of, and damage to, the components of any parts of plumbing, central heating and drainage systems can lead to water leakage. If a persistent leakage problem exists fungal decay may develop. Particular attention should be paid to inspection of those areas where water leaks might occur and go unnoticed for long periods. Areas where typical defects may be found which lead to water leakage are:

Typical signs of plumbing defects: leakage around a rainwater down pipe (above) and plaster fungi around leaking domestic plumbing

❏ water supply pipes under suspended ground floors

❏ areas beneath and around baths (especially panelled baths), shower cubicles, basins, sinks and toilets, central heating radiators and valves, hot water cylinders, and in airing cupboards

❏ ceilings, floors and areas beneath hot and cold water, central heating and waste pipe runs, particularly at joints and changes of direction

❏ pipes inside ducting, particularly uninsulated pipes on which condensation may occur

❏ internal rainwater downpipes and internal soil pipes where they pass through timber floors

❏ open rainwater gutters inside roof voids (older buildings)

Detection of decayed timbers

The symptoms of severe decay in exposed timbers will usually be obvious. **However, some decayed timbers retain a surface veneer of sound wood. It is important, therefore, to thoroughly investigate all suspect timbers adjacent to actual or potential sources of dampness, and any showing evidence of fungal growths.** This may be done by probing with a sharp implement such as a bradawl; the presence of internal decay in large-section timbers can often be detected by 'sounding' with a hammer (see page 28). In particular, careful probing is required where timbers, such as joist ends and roof purlins, enter walls since decay can be localised in the portions of timber embedded in the masonry. All timbers showing substantial deterioration due to fungal decay must be noted for replacement or repair; fungal softening (eg, brash fracturing of splinters levered from the surface with a probe) indicates the early stages of decay and should also be considered for remedial action.

Probing for evidence of decay: the long splinters found when timber is rot-free (above) and the short brash splinters which indicate that the timber has been attacked by wood-rotting fungi

In many cases, decayed timber will be obvious during the initial visual inspection; for example, with decayed wall plates or truss ends in the eaves of a pitched roof. However, decay often occurs in timbers hidden from view, such as ground floor joists in poorly ventilated situations or timbers built tightly into masonry. Therefore, some opening up of the building

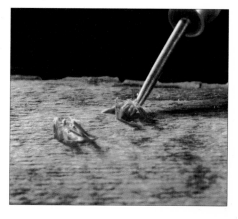

structure is usually necessary to allow inspection of hidden timbers. Particular attention must be given to hidden timbers adjacent to sources of dampness, external or internal, detected during the inspection. (The figures on this page show examples of opening up.)

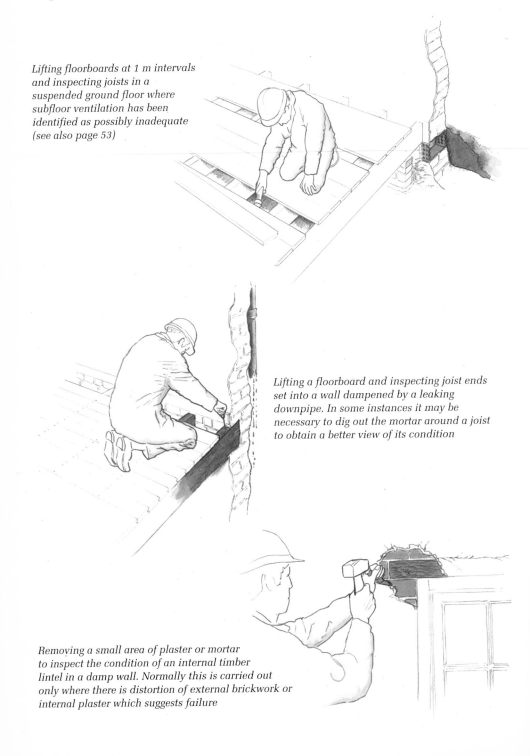

Lifting floorboards at 1 m intervals and inspecting joists in a suspended ground floor where subfloor ventilation has been identified as possibly inadequate (see also page 53)

Lifting a floorboard and inspecting joist ends set into a wall dampened by a leaking downpipe. In some instances it may be necessary to dig out the mortar around a joist to obtain a better view of its condition

Removing a small area of plaster or mortar to inspect the condition of an internal timber lintel in a damp wall. Normally this is carried out only where there is distortion of external brickwork or internal plaster which suggests failure

Identifying sound timbers at risk

Timbers which are damp but show little or no decay, and which are still fulfilling their structural function, may be retained provided that they can be dried out sufficiently rapidly to prevent significant further decay (ie, dried to 20% moisture content or below). Where drying will be more delayed, application of wood preservatives may be appropriate.

The timber surveyor must therefore use his experience and judgement to estimate the likely drying times for damp timbers. Such estimates should take into account the measures introduced to remove sources of moisture, the introduction of heating and ventilation regimes, the extent of dampness in the timbers and adjacent masonry as assessed by moisture meter readings, and the thickness of the damp timber and masonry.

Estimates of drying times can allow the surveyor to categorise timbers in terms of their remedial needs. For example:

❏ timbers likely to dry rapidly (within about eight weeks) and which therefore require no additional measures. In the main, timbers out of contact with masonry, and subject to free air movement around at least three sides, will dry fairly rapidly

❏ timbers likely to take up to six months to dry out and which therefore require temporary protection, usually in the form of in situ treatment with wood preservatives (see page 57). Timbers in this category are typically in contact with, or embedded in, masonry which has been subjected to temporary and localised dampness, the source of which can be readily removed

❏ timbers likely to remain damp for a year or more, therefore requiring modifications to remove them from contact with dampness or, as a last resort, replacement with a more durable substitute such as concrete or steel. Timbers in this category are typically in contact with, or embedded in, damp masonry which cannot be dried rapidly

In a case of doubt, it is usually safer to err on the side of caution with respect to estimation of drying times, and therefore to over rather than underestimate the need for positive drying or other remedial measures. Where a building can be revisited at intervals (eg, in large buildings undergoing extensive renovation), the moisture content of suspect timbers can be checked at intervals to assess whether drying is progressing as planned.

Inspection for insect attack in timber

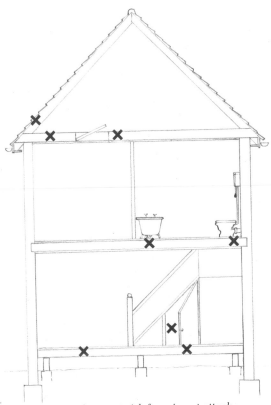

Typical areas of greatest risk from insect attack

Wood-boring insect damage in a building may vary from widespread to highly localised attack. The species of insect responsible must be identified (see Table 5.1 on page 50) and a thorough building inspection carried out to establish the extent and severity of attack, and whether it is still active (see Table 7.1 on page 68). Ideally, all timbers should be examined, particularly those in areas likely to have been subjected to persistent dampness (eg, suspended ground floors, roof voids, bathroom and toilet floors, and cupboards beneath stairs on ground floors).

However, where there are severe constraints on access, sampling of the less accessible timbers, such as floor joists, may be warranted provided the limitations of this approach are understood by all concerned.

Visual inspection for emergence holes is the usual method of detecting infestation. A strong light and access to roof voids and subfloor spaces are obvious additional requirements. A list of useful equipment will be found in Chapter 3.

Assessing the significance of detected damage

Although most insects feeding on standing trees and felled logs in the forest die out as the timber is dried prior to use, their tunnels remain and may subsequently be confused with those of wood-boring insects for which remedial treatment is needed. Similarly, those which feed exclusively on damp decayed wood or in bark require no further treatment than that necessary to deal with associated fungal decay or the mechanical removal of the infected bark. If unnecessary treatment is to be avoided, it is important that insect damage in building timbers should be correctly identified and classified.

Table 5.1(overleaf) classifies insects into three damage categories:

❑ preservative treatment usually needed

❑ treatment necessary only to control associated wood rot

❑ no treatment needed

Assessing the structural significance of insect attack

Most infestations of common furniture beetle, even of long standing, are of little structural significance and therefore require little or no replacement of timber. Probing with a sharp instrument to remove powdered wood will usually determine the extent of damage.

House longhorn beetle infestations commonly cause structural damage, particularly where the timbers affected contain a large proportion of sapwood. In buildings constructed from about 1920 onwards, damage can be significant, but in older buildings where timbers tend to contain lower proportions of sapwood, the significance of damage is usually less. Damage needs to be assessed by thorough probing, drilling or sounding as the house longhorn beetle usually leaves a sound skin of wood over the damaged timber.

Attack by deathwatch beetle can be more difficult to assess for structural damage as it is often localised in built-in timbers such as joist ends, or exists as hidden cavities of deterioration in the centres of large timbers. Surface probing should therefore be augmented by rigorous probing of timbers where they enter potentially damp walls, by 'sounding' with a hammer, and by drilling into large timbers showing evidence of exit holes not associated with sapwood edges.

Damage by Lyctus powderpost beetle normally falls into two categories. In properties more than about 20 years old, any damage will be extinct due to natural depletion of the starch content of the timber on which the beetle depends. Such damage is common on the sapwood edges of large-section hardwood beams in older properties and is generally of no structural significance. In more modern properties, damage to hardwood fittings and plywood components may be severe and usually require replacement.

Weevil infestations of decayed damp timber require no specific remedial measures beyond those necessary to eradicate the fungal decay. Very extensive infestations may cause temporary annoyance to building occupants when adult beetles leave the drying timber and invade inhabited rooms.

Damage by Ptilinus beetle is only occasionally encountered in buildings, and then only in hardwoods. Assessment and significance is identical to those for common furniture beetle.

Table 5.1 Recognising common wood-boring insects

Type of borer	Recognition of damage	
	Habitat	Emergence hole shape and size (mm)
Damage for which remedial treatment is usually needed		
Common furniture beetle	Sapwood of softwoods and European hardwoods	Circular 1 – 2
Ptilinus beetle	Limited number of European hardwoods	Circular 1 – 2
House longhorn beetle	Sapwood of softwoods	Oval 6 – 10 often ragged
Lyctus powderpost beetle	Sapwood of coarse-pored hardwoods	Circular 1.5
Deathwatch beetle	Sapwood and heartwood of decayed hardwoods, occasionally softwoods	Circular 3
Damage for which remedial treatment is necessary only to control associated wood rot		
Wood-boring weevil	Any, if damp and decayed	Ragged 1
Wharf borer beetle	Any, if damp and decayed	Oval 6
Leaf cutter bee / solitary wasp	Any, if badly decayed	Circular 6
Damage for which no remedial treatment is needed		
Pinhole borer beetles	Any in log form	Circular 1 – 2
Bark borer beetle	Bark of softwoods	Circular 1.5 – 2 some in bark, few in sapwood
Wood wasp	Sapwood and heartwood of softwoods	Circular 4 – 7
Forest longhorn beetles	Any	Oval 6 – 10 on bark edges only; may be larger in some hardwoods
Marine borers	Any	None, but tunnel sections can be exposed by sawing

Table 5.1   Recognising common wood-boring insects *(continued)*

Recognition of damage *(continued)*	
Tunnels	**Bore dust**
Damage for which remedial treatment is usually needed	
Numerous, close	Cream, granular, lemon-shaped pellets (× 10 lens)
Numerous, close	Pink or cream talc-like, not easily dislodged from tunnels
Numerous, often coalesce to powdery mass beneath the surface veneer	Cream powder, chips and cylindrical pellets
Numerous, close	Cream, talc-like
Numerous, close, eventually forming a honeycomb appearance	Brown, disc-shaped pellets
Damage for which remedial treatment is necessary only to control associated wood rot	
Numerous, close, breaking through to surface in places	Brown, fine, lemon-shaped pellets (× 10 lens)
Numerous, close, often coalescing to form cavities	Dark brown, mud-like substance; bundles of coarse wood fibres
Sparse network	Brown chips, metallic-like fragments, fly wings, barrel-shaped cocoons of leaves
Damage for which no remedial treatment is needed	
Across grain, darkly stained	None
Network between bark and few in sapwood	Cream and brown round pellets underlying wood
Few, widely spaced	Coarse, powdery
Few, widely spread; sections on sawn surfaces oval 6 – 10 mm	None or, rarely, small piles of coarse fibres
Circular up to 15 mm	None, but tunnels may have white chalky lining

6 Remedial treatment of fungal decay

The early sections of this chapter deal with the general measures necessary to eradicate fungal decay, whether it is dry rot or of the wet rot type. Dry rot presents particular problems for the treatment contractor, requiring special measures which are also described in this chapter.

Having identified the sources of excessive dampness in a building, the next stage is to rectify the causes. This requires only conventional building repair works such as the replacement of defective rainwater goods or roof flashings, or the installation of air bricks in walls. Performance of these works is outside the scope of this book. **However, it is vital to understand that, until the works are completed, any other actions to remedy dampness and its consequences will be ineffective and a waste of time and resources.**

Drying the building fabric

Once the sources of water entry identified by the inspection have been eliminated, the damp building fabric needs to be dried out. The rate of progress of any timber decay will then begin to decline and will stop altogether when the timber moisture content falls to below about 22%. In order to prevent any significant spread of decay during this drying period, it is essential that drying is achieved as rapidly as is practicable.

In lightweight constructions where dampness, and therefore decay, has been localised, rapid drying can normally be achieved by maintaining heating and ventilation within rooms and unoccupied voids, such as roofs and beneath suspended ground floors, at levels consistent with those for normal occupancy. In heavier constructions and where dampness has been widespread or severe, extra temporary measures to speed the drying process will be needed.

Ventilation

In many cases of severe dampness and subsequent decay, considerable opening up of voids by removing floorboards and ceiling plaster will be necessary to effect repairs to timbers. Complete reinstatement of these should be delayed as long as is practicable so as to promote air movement around damp joists, etc. Leaving a floorboard lifted at each side of a room will increase air flow around joists, particularly where they are set into masonry.

In conjunction with temporarily accelerated ventilation of voids, free air flow through a building can be further increased by opening a window in each room and leaving connecting doors between rooms open. Chimney flues should also be left unobstructed to allow air movement.

In buildings undergoing extensive and lengthy refurbishment, or those likely to remain unoccupied and unheated for some time following remedial work, natural ventilation can be further improved by temporary replacement of some windows with louvred grilles which will also provide some security against unauthorised entry. These grilles will need to incorporate 10 mm metal mesh screens to exclude birds.

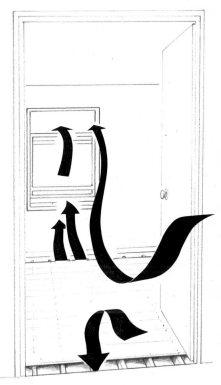

Measures to be taken for the temporary ventilation of flooring timbers

Heating

Temporarily raised heating levels in a building will also speed the drying of timbers. However, it is important that through ventilation is also maintained: air into which water has evaporated from damp surfaces must be allowed to escape from the building. Failure to ensure adequate ventilation during a period of heating could result in condensation occurring on colder surfaces which previously had been dry.

Such heating is best achieved using existing flued heating systems, or electric heaters. Unflued gas or paraffin space heaters must be used with great caution as they produce large quantities of water and must therefore be used only in conjunction with very effective ventilation.

SAFETY FACTORS TO BE CONSIDERED WHEN USING HEATING APPLIANCES IN ENCLOSED AREAS

Gas, coal and paraffin-burning heating appliances need a plentiful supply of air if they are to operate efficiently. **An inadequate supply of air, which might be found for instance in an enclosed space, leads to incomplete combustion and the production of carbon monoxide. This is an odourless and invisible but lethal gas.**

Therefore, those situations in which the air supply to a fuel-burning appliance might be restricted should be avoided. For example, the doors and windows to an enclosed and unventilated area in which it is proposed to use one of these heating appliances must be opened up to allow proper ventilation. (Such ventilation is likely, anyway to aid drying more readily than heating.)

Where a powerful extract fan is also used with a combustion appliance, allowance must be made for the extra fresh air supplies to satisfy both heating and ventilation requirements.

Dehumidifiers

Where temporary ventilation of damp rooms or voids by natural means is not feasible (eg, for reasons of security), dehumidifiers can be used to speed up drying times.

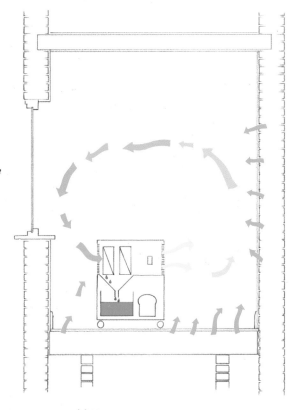

Dehumidifiers extract moisture from the air and, by creating dry air in a room or void, increase the drying rate of timber exposed to the air. Their performance, though, is critically dependent on the temperature and humidity conditions under which they are operated. They will perform well in well heated areas with high moisture levels, but not so well if the areas are poorly heated and are not effectively sealed against the outside air. Furthermore, they must have sufficient capacity to extract at least about three litres of water per day; small capacity models make little difference to humidity levels. The container holding the water (condensate) must be emptied regularly or routed to a domestic waste outlet.

Monitoring of drying

Because buildings differ radically in design as well as in the degrees and patterns of dampness which may be present, no mention has been made so far of specific ventilation rates or heating levels.

Drying regimes are normally decided by a combination of experience and trial and error. In order to determine whether a drying regime is achieving results or needs to be increased, generally or in specific areas, monitoring is essential. This can only be carried out by regularly measuring the moisture content of specific timbers using a moisture meter (see pages 25 and 26 for guidance on use).

Ideally, a record should be kept of regular readings taken at the same positions on a range of timbers, including the dampest elements or sections such as joist ends or wall plates in direct contact with masonry. In large complex buildings, permanently installed measuring probes linked to centralised recording equipment are increasingly being used to monitor moisture levels during renovation and to provide early warning of the need for maintenance.

Protecting retained timbers during drying

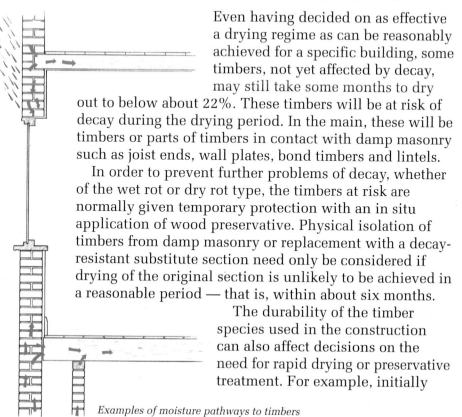

Even having decided on as effective a drying regime as can be reasonably achieved for a specific building, some timbers, not yet affected by decay, may still take some months to dry out to below about 22%. These timbers will be at risk of decay during the drying period. In the main, these will be timbers or parts of timbers in contact with damp masonry such as joist ends, wall plates, bond timbers and lintels.

In order to prevent further problems of decay, whether of the wet rot or dry rot type, the timbers at risk are normally given temporary protection with an in situ application of wood preservative. Physical isolation of timbers from damp masonry or replacement with a decay-resistant substitute section need only be considered if drying of the original section is unlikely to be achieved in a reasonable period — that is, within about six months.

The durability of the timber species used in the construction can also affect decisions on the need for rapid drying or preservative treatment. For example, initially

Examples of moisture pathways to timbers

sound oak heartwood joists and lintels can remain damp for several years before any risk of significant decay occurs. But most softwood timbers, whether heartwood or sapwood, are generally at risk of decay where drying is delayed beyond a few weeks.

Isolation techniques

Any method can be used which provides a break in the moisture pathway between damp masonry and timber (see figures below and steel joist-end extension on next page). The only limitations are those imposed by cost and the need to retain structural integrity. **Before embarking on such measures, the advice of a qualified structural engineer should be sought as to the effects of proposed modifications.**

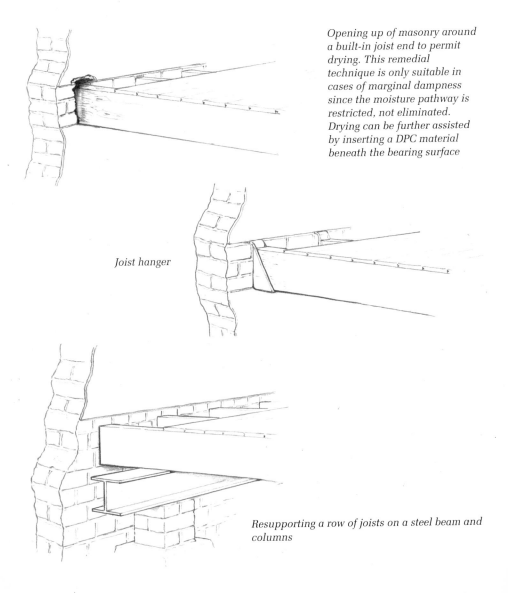

Opening up of masonry around a built-in joist end to permit drying. This remedial technique is only suitable in cases of marginal dampness since the moisture pathway is restricted, not eliminated. Drying can be further assisted by inserting a DPC material beneath the bearing surface

Joist hanger

Resupporting a row of joists on a steel beam and columns

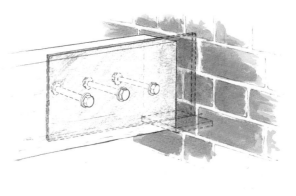

Steel joist-end extension (eg, flitch beam)

Preservative treatment techniques

The circumstances in which in situ applications of remedial timber preservatives may be appropriate are detailed in Table 6.1 (overleaf), a decision tree based on the particular scenarios which the surveyor may encounter.

If in situ treatments with preservative are to provide significant protection of drying timbers, they must penetrate deeply into the wood. Brushing or spraying will not provide the necessary degree of penetration and cannot be applied to surfaces embedded in masonry. They will only provide, therefore, limited superficial protection against decay.

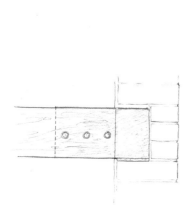

Improved penetration of preservative in situ can be provided by pressure injection with liquid preservatives (see figure on left). Non-pressure application of liquids into holes drilled in timber is also practised but should be limited to large-section timbers. Penetrating pastes, applied to small areas of damp timbers, are also widely used (see figure on page 59). Systems based on drilling of timbers and insertion of solid sticks

Pressure injection with liquid preservatives

Table 6.1   A suggested method for deciding whether remedial treatment against fungal attack is justified

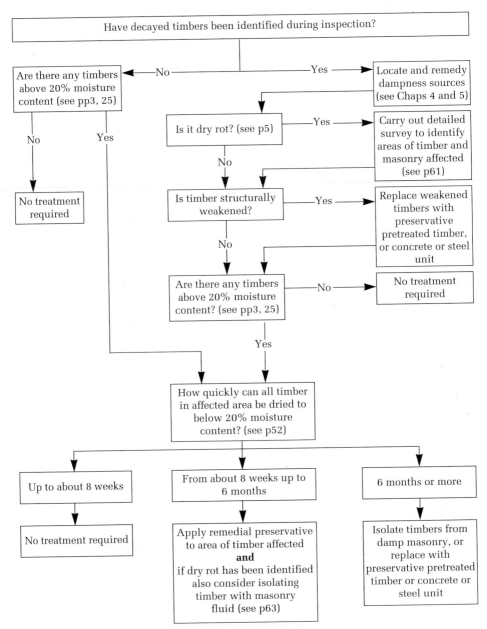

of diffusible wood preservative (see figure on next page) are available and are becoming more popular for offering protection in such situations as joist ends set into damp brickwork.

Preservative treatment need not be extended beyond those timbers or parts of timbers which are likely to be at risk of further decay as a

Applying penetrating paste

result of delayed drying. This would typically apply only to timbers directly in contact with damp masonry and extending about 300 mm from the contact area. Beyond this point, drying of timbers exposed to free air movement can usually be achieved within a sufficiently short period to prevent any further significant decay.

Only where currently dry timber is at particular risk of future accidental wetting (eg, a plate beneath a valley gutter) can in situ preservative treatment of the timber be justified on the basis of giving some limited protection against the decay risks arising from future temporary wetting before the building defect is rectified.

Attempts to protect timbers which are likely to remain damp indefinitely by means of in situ surface treatment with preservatives are likely to fail and therefore could result in the need for more substantial remedial work at some future date.

Inserting a solid stick of diffusible wood preservative into a joist end

WARNING ON THE TREATMENT OF DAMP TIMBER

The brush or spray treatment of damp timbers with wood preservative will provide protection only to a superficial layer of wood; it is therefore of little value in preventing further decay of already infected timber which remains damp indefinitely. It may even temporarily disguise the evidence of continuing deep seated decay.

WINDOW JOINERY, CLADDING AND OTHER EXTERNAL TIMBERS

Unless protected by roof overhangs or deep reveals, window joinery and other exposed timbers on the outside of buildings can be subjected to persistent wetting by rain or snow. Paint films do not give complete protection against moisture penetration and may even encourage persistently high moisture content by preventing the drying of moisture which has entered timber through cracks in the paint film. It can be assumed, then, that many external timbers will exceed the threshold for decay for considerable periods

Inserting a solid stick of diffusible wood preservative into a window frame

and be at severe risk of decay. It is normally necessary, therefore, for external timbers to be either preservative pretreated or prepared from naturally durable timber.

Components manufactured from timbers of low natural durability will have a short service life under severe exposure conditions. Decay, which can be detected by careful probing, is most commonly found in the bottom joints of window frames; exposed end-grain is particularly susceptible to water penetration. Replacement of severely decayed frames is often the most cost-effective solution.

The life of lightly decayed frames can be extended by a combination of spliced repairs and, for bottom joints which are still reasonably sound, either:

❑ in situ injection of preservative, or

❑ insertion of solid sticks of diffusible wood preservative (see photograph above)

The former requires the services of a specialist contractor using pressure equipment. The latter method is available to both the specialist and the non-specialist.

Dry rot

Determining the extent of infection

Although dry rot requires the same minimum moisture level as wet rots to cause decay in timber and is therefore restricted to damp areas, it is able to grow through permeable masonry materials such as plaster and mortar. As this ability to grow through masonry allows relatively rapid spread through damp or poorly ventilated parts of a structure, it is important that the full extent of infection is identified and any timbers in contact with the affected masonry are adequately protected until drying is finished or, if necessary, removed.

Although full stripping of plaster from affected walls does allow the extent of fungal growth on the underlying masonry to be assessed, the disruption and cost of this exercise is not necessarily justified. Limited stripping of plaster in selected areas, such as around joist ends and door frames, to determine the presence and condition of timber lintels and bond timbers, is often adequate. The decision on the scale of stripping necessary is a matter for the professional surveyor on the basis of his experience and site conditions. It should be remembered that the fungus does no harm to masonry and the emphasis should be, therefore, on identifying timbers which are in direct contact with infected masonry.

In assessing the extent of the dry rot, great care must be taken to plot the area affected by dampness (see page 26). All timbers in contact with the area of masonry identified as damp should be carefully examined for evidence of decay, particularly those in or forming poorly ventilated voids — for instance, under floors, and in enclosed roof eaves, internal panelling, sash weight boxes, pipe casings, cellars and basements.

Treatment of dry rot

Once the full extent of dampness and decay has been determined, the basic strategy of control by drying should be applied as described earlier in this chapter. In cases where thorough drying can be achieved rapidly, this strategy alone will be sufficient.

However, where rapid drying cannot be guaranteed there is the possibility of a period of continued, although limited, spread of the fungus through masonry. If the fungus then comes into contact with poorly ventilated timbers, or marginally damp timbers coated with impervious paint films (eg, gloss painted panelling), these could be attacked also.

In order to minimise this possibility of further decay, the following measures should be taken.

MISCONCEPTIONS ABOUT DRY ROT AND MOISTURE

Dry rot can transport its own water sufficiently to cause extensive spread to drier parts of a building

Although the strands and mycelia of dry rot can transport water, their capacity to do this is limited. The fungus can only spread from damp areas into adjacent areas where ventilation is so restricted that the transported moisture can build up and promote decay in the wetted timbers. Gloss paints and other impervious coatings on masonry or stud walls act as barriers to water vapour, and may allow the fungus to dampen the underlying wall and so enable it to spread.

Dry rot can remain dormant for many years and then suddenly induce a new outbreak

Dry rot mycelia and strands can remain inactive in dry timber for many years before finally dying, especially under cooler conditions such as in cellars. However, only if damp conditions return, exceeding 22% moisture content, will the fungus become sufficiently active for significant spread to occur; for example, where untreated timber of low natural durability remains in contact with either infected timber or masonry containing infected timber fragments. Although dry rot can survive in a dormant state in dry masonry for some time, it is not known for how long.

❑ Limiting the source of food for the fungus by removing, wherever possible, any non-essential timber components (including fixing blocks and similar items) in contact with the area of masonry which has been identified as both damp and infected. Where such timbers are replaced, then more durable substitutes must be used.

❑ Identifying and providing permanent ventilation of timbers in poorly ventilated voids.

❑ Extending the isolation and preservative treatment of damp timbers to all timbers, **whether damp or not**, set into masonry close to areas which have been identified as damp and infected with the fungus. The maximum distance from damp infected areas which constitute a possible risk of spread of the fungus will vary, and is dependent on factors such as the degree of dampness and the speed of the drying. Typically a distance of about 500 mm is used. Alternatively, isolating timbers within about 500 mm of damp infected masonry by treatment with a water-based fungicide (dry rot masonry fluid) as a

MISCONCEPTIONS ABOUT TREATMENT OF DRY ROT

Effective dry rot control requires all infected timber to be removed and all infected masonry to be sterilised

Although removal or sterilisation of infected material would in theory achieve control, in practice it is often impossible to identify precisely all infection and impracticable to remove or sterilise all affected material. The essence of effective control is the prompt restoration and future maintenance of dry conditions.

Infected and decayed wood removed from a building should be treated with preservative or burnt on site

As a matter of good practice infected timber should be removed from any building with damp conditions. However, once removed it can be temporarily and safely stored outside on site provided that it is not adjacent to the walls of any buildings. Disposal to a local authority site poses no hazards, although contamination of hardcore with decayed wood can lead to decay problems in new construction. Treated wood might be regarded by local authorities as toxic waste and unauthorised disposal to a landfill site therefore could be illegal. Burning infected, untreated timber on site is common practice but it is not necessary as a means of removing any decay risk to existing buildings.

Dry rot spores on oversites beneath suspended timber ground floors must be sterilised by spraying with dry rot masonry fluid

Dry rot spores on an oversite cannot result in the spread of the fungus unless timber, card or paper debris are present on or in the oversite. If such debris is present in an infected building, it may well already be infected and must be removed. Surface spraying of the oversite is unlikely to prevent the spread of fungus from infected debris and, except under unusual circumstances, is unlikely to be justifiable as a result of a COSHH assessment (see page 85).

band about 300–450 mm wide through the depth of the masonry (see figure overleaf).

This latter method is less satisfactory as in some masonry it cannot be guaranteed to provide a complete barrier to further fungal growth. Its use should be minimised, in any case, since the treatment is water-based and therefore further delays drying.

In addition to these measures, it has been common practice to spray dry rot masonry fluids onto damp infected wall surfaces to prevent the appearance of dry rot fruit-bodies which commonly appear during drying and may disrupt old and new plasterwork. In the interests of reducing the amounts of fungicide introduced, such treatments should be restricted to those areas of masonry where there is clear evidence of dampness and substantial infection.

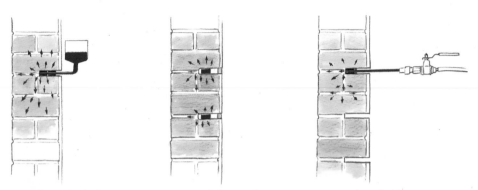

Principle methods for treating masonry with fungicide: non-pressure reservoir (left); pressure injection; diffusible plug (right)

Repairs to decayed timber

Extent of removal

Ideally as much damp decayed timber should be removed from a building as is practicable in order to reduce the possibility of further spread during drying. This is particularly so in the case of dry rot where damp, decaying timber can provide a source for spread of the fungus through adjacent damp masonry. In the case of a decayed joist end, for example, it is normal to cut out the decayed section together with about 300 mm of adjacent sound wood, although site conditions may on occasions require larger areas to be removed.

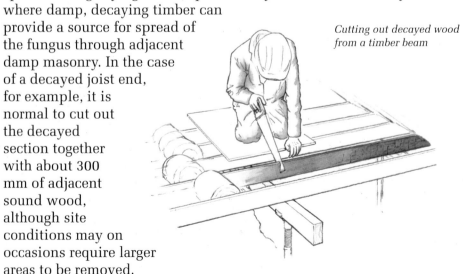

Cutting out decayed wood from a timber beam

It is also good practice to remove any visible fungal growths, mycelium and fruit-bodies from timber and masonry surfaces. This will minimise the extent of further growth and will enable assessment of the extent of any continued fungal activity to be made more easily. Following a COSHH assessment, it will probably be necessary for a filter-type face mask to be worn during treatment operations.

In some situations it may be too costly, or unacceptable for conservation reasons, to remove all timbers showing symptoms of decay. Under these circumstances the remaining decayed material presents a degree of risk only until drying has been completed. To minimise continued risk, the application of penetrating in situ preservative can be used as described earlier. Dry decayed timbers present no risk of further decay. If partially decayed timbers are retained, it is essential to ensure that they retain adequate structural strength. In a temporarily damp situation, the degree of risk associated with retaining a timber section with a decayed sapwood edge will be significantly lower for a more durable timber species, such as European oak, than for a more perishable one.

Specification for replacements

Replacement with materials such as steel or reinforced concrete is sometimes the most practicable solution for decayed timber lintels or bond timbers, particularly where rapid drying of the masonry into which they are set cannot be guaranteed. Where replacement timber is to be used, good building practice requires that it should be pretreated with an appropriate preservative to protect against decay arising from residual dampness as well as against the possibility of a recurrence of the building defect leading to the original cause of decay. It should also be isolated from masonry as far as is practicable and not built into unventilated voids.

Timber which has been pretreated by a pressure-vacuum process is to be preferred, although brush treatment of ends cut on site with a wood preservative solution as recommended by the supplier of the treated timber is also necessary. Where dampness will not persist, organic solvent preservatives applied by the double vacuum process are suitable (British Standard BS 5707:Part 1[3] gives details). Where dampness may persist a pressure-impregnated preservative of the copper-chromium-arsenic type is necessary (BS 4072:Part 2[4] gives details). BS 5268:Part 5[5] gives detailed specifications for preservative pretreatment of structural timbers in specific locations in buildings.

European Standards currently in draft form will provide different procedures for specifying the performance of treated wood with respect to particular hazard classes. These hazard classes will include situations in which timbers are subjected to persistent or intermittent dampness. In the future, therefore, treated timbers will be marked as suitable for particular hazard classes.

Replacement of decayed timbers with timber of high natural durability is an alternative, though it can be expensive compared to replacement with other materials. It requires, also, careful selection to avoid inclusion of non-durable sapwood. More durable species include European oak, Douglas fir, western red cedar, chestnut, iroko*, utile* and opepe*.

---

* The use of tropical hardwoods, such as iroko, utile and opepe, from certain environmentally sensitive sources is generally considered undesirable. A contractor considering using a hardwood is advised to establish whether it has been obtained from regulated, well-managed sources, and then consult with his client about the choice of timber, taking into account any environmental policies which the client may have.

7 Remedial treatment of wood-boring insect attack

Application of a remedial preservative should be considered only after insect damage has been identified as:

❑ of a type requiring treatment; that is, due to attack by common furniture beetle, house longhorn beetle or deathwatch beetle (or less frequently by Lyctus powderpost beetle, wood-boring weevils or Ptilinus beetle) (see Table 5.1 on page 50)

❑ also that it is active, or there is a significant risk of activity (see Table 7.1 overleaf)

The type of treatment necessary will depend on the particular insect species identified as well as the severity of attack (see Table 7.2 on page 69).

Types of preservative treatment

When selecting a remedial wood preservative for use against wood-boring insects, it is important the user establishes that the product is intended for this specific purpose. Some preservatives are intended solely for control of fungal decay.

Two main types of remedial wood preservative for control of wood-boring insects are available, both liquids:

❑ organic solvent-based products

❑ emulsion-based (water-based) products

Table 7.1 A structured approach to deciding whether remedial treatment against insect attack is justified

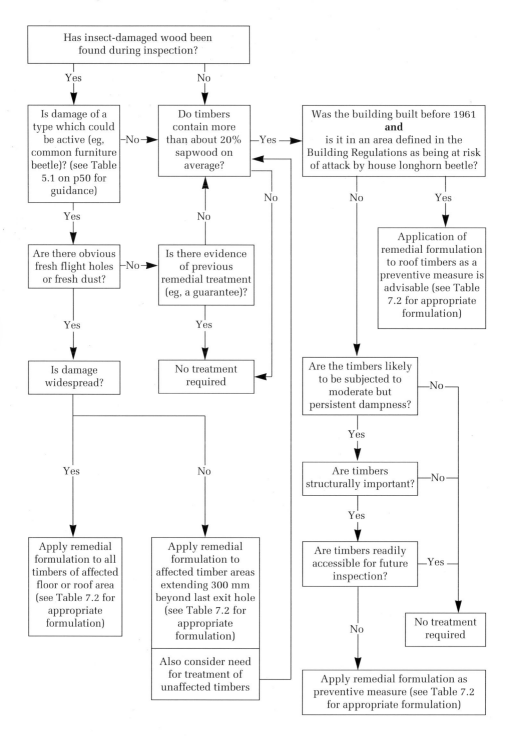

Table 7.2 Selecting the remedial preservative product and method of application for treatment of wood-boring insect attack

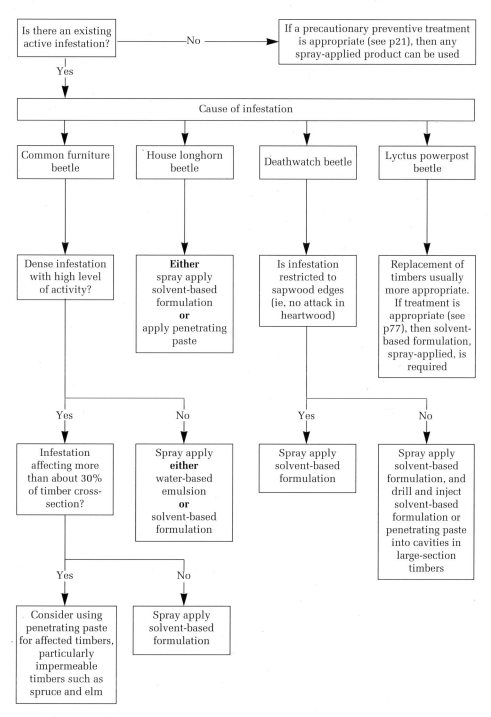

Note: where more than one type of treatment is suitable, COSHH considerations dictate that the least hazardous product should be used

These products contain similar types and levels of active insecticide, but most emulsion-based products penetrate less deeply than solvent-based types and are suitable only for use against light infestations of the less structurally damaging common furniture beetle*. Both types penetrate into the timber and kill some larvae (grubs) more or less immediately. In subsequent years, the surviving larvae mature into insects which are only then killed by residual insecticide as they bore their way to the surface. Solvent-based products kill more larvae than simple emulsion-based types at the time of application simply because they penetrate further into the infected timber.

Paste products can give deep penetration but are not suitable for widespread application and are more costly.

Further, more detailed descriptions of these and other treatment products are given on pages 71–75.

All of these products must be applied in strict accordance with instructions on the manufacturers' labels (see pages 82–85) and only after completion of a COSHH assessment (see page 85). In the case of a localised infestation, preservative treatment should not, generally, need to extend more than about 300 mm beyond the evidence of activity shown by exit holes. The justification for treatment beyond the area of timber showing exit holes will depend on particular circumstances (Table 7.1 gives detailed guidance).

Since only a small proportion of insects in an infestation come to the timber surface each spring or summer, there are no significant benefits in applying the wood preservative at any particular time of year.

Spray application is normally adopted as the most convenient method of delivering a preservative product to timber surfaces. However, it should be appreciated that there are **no** benefits in the use of a high pressure atomised spray as it will achieve no better penetration of timber than a low pressure coarse spray. There are significant safety hazards, though, in using an atomised spray (see page 99).

The following describes the full range of liquid and other insecticidal treatments currently available.

---

* At the time of printing, new developments within the preservative manufacturing industry were yielding emulsions which penetrate more effectively including products referred to as micro-emulsion systems. It seems likely that these will be able to overcome some of the limitations of traditional emulsions. However, contractors should seek the assurance of manufacturers on the suitability of these new products for specific uses.

Liquid treatments

These are the most commonly used, each consisting of a suitably long-lasting (persistent) contact insecticide dissolved in a carrier fluid. A range of insecticides and carriers are available, but all are intended to:

❏ kill insects already within the timber by penetrating the timber and killing larvae in the zone of penetration (initial kill)

❏ leave a persistent layer of insecticide in the zone penetrated which kills insects surviving the initial kill as they tunnel to the surface as adults

❏ prevent further infestation and so protect timber against future damage by leaving a persistent layer of insecticide in the zone penetrated to kill any eggs or hatching larvae

The effectiveness of different liquid treatments in achieving these objectives depends on the formulation, on the size and permeability of the infested timbers, and on the thoroughness of application.

Organic solvent-based products

Sometimes referred to as spirit-based or oil-based, these products consist of persistent contact insecticides dissolved in a volatile carrier fluid such as white spirit. They are usually applied to the surface of the wood by spray or brush at recommended rates of 200–300 ml/m². With sapwood of permeable timbers, Scots pine (redwood) for instance, penetration on lateral surfaces of up to 10 mm can be expected. Larvae within this zone are killed immediately by the combined effects of the solvent and the insecticide. In less permeable timbers, spruce and oak for example, penetration is reduced and a smaller proportion of larvae will be killed initially. In some cases, particularly with large-dimension timbers, penetration of treatment fluid may be improved by injection under pressure through one-way valve inserts or slow irrigation into drilled holes.

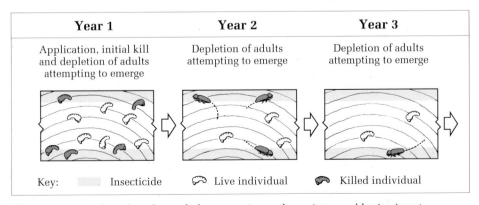

Year 1	Year 2	Year 3
Application, initial kill and depletion of adults attempting to emerge	Depletion of adults attempting to emerge	Depletion of adults attempting to emerge

Key: ▢ Insecticide   🪱 Live individual   🪱 Killed individual

How an organic solvent-based remedial preservative works against wood-boring insects

Emulsion-based (water-based) products

These formulations consist of an emulsified mixture of water and organic solvent in which the insecticide is carried in the organic solvent phase. The ratio of organic solvent:water varies considerably between products but is typically about 1:10. Formulations based entirely on water as a carrier cannot be produced because the insecticides currently used in remedial timber treatments are insoluble in water. Emulsion fluids can be applied only by spray or brush; because of their high water content, injection could cause swelling of the timber. There are many formulations but current evidence suggests that those based on organic solvent:water ratios of about 1:10 tend to achieve relatively shallow penetration of insecticide compared with organic solvent-based treatments, even in permeable timbers. Their effectiveness is therefore more dependent on the action of insecticide in the residual zone against emerging adults and newly-laid eggs rather than on a high initial kill of larvae. This implies that larval activity (and, with highly active attacks, significant structural damage) may continue for possibly several years after treatment.

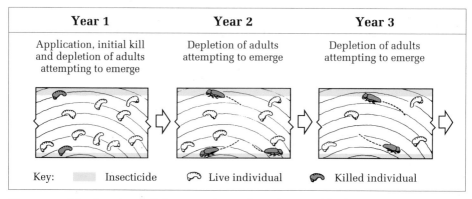

Year 1	Year 2	Year 3
Application, initial kill and depletion of adults attempting to emerge	Depletion of adults attempting to emerge	Depletion of adults attempting to emerge

Key: ▢ Insecticide   ⌒ Live individual   ⌒ Killed individual

How an emulsion-based remedial preservative works against wood-boring insects

Paste products (bodied emulsions)

These consist of the same contact insecticides which are incorporated in liquid formulations but carried in a gelatinous emulsion paste with a high oil-solvent content; typical recommended application rates are 600–800 ml/m^2. Their main characteristic is that they adhere to wood surfaces and deliver greater quantities of active ingredients than liquids which are limited by run-off; they therefore have a potential for greater loadings and deeper penetration of insecticide and solvent. Their main disadvantages are:

❑ longer times to apply the paste (either by caulking gun or pallet knife)

❏ a tendency to leave a waxy deposit or skin on the wood surface after absorption of the paste

❏ the risk of staining adjacent plaster

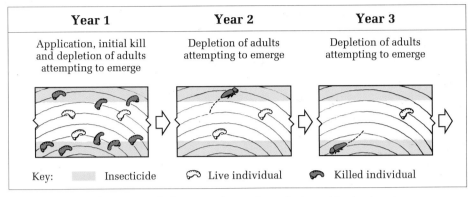

Year 1	Year 2	Year 3
Application, initial kill and depletion of adults attempting to emerge	Depletion of adults attempting to emerge	Depletion of adults attempting to emerge

Key:　　　Insecticide　　　Live individual　　　Killed individual

How an insecticidal paste remedial preservative works against wood-boring insects

Smoke treatments

Low cost pyrotechnic canisters can be used to produce clouds of insecticidal particles in the form of smoke. When released in a building or a void within a building, the smoke will deposit a fine layer of insecticide on all surfaces (including vertical surfaces and the undersides of timbers). The surface deposits will kill all crawling insects which come into contact with the insecticide, provided the application rate is adequate.

The smoke deposits kill only beetles, eggs and hatching larvae on surfaces and cannot affect larvae in the wood. Control is achieved by preventing egg-laying and reinfestation by emerging beetles, so gradually reducing the numbers of larvae remaining in the wood. This form of treatment is cheaper than liquid types and can be useful on impermeable timbers where penetration by liquids is difficult to achieve. It is also easier to use in buildings with large amounts of timber which are inaccessible without scaffolding. The limitations of smoke treatments are that:

❏ effective control requires repeated annual treatments, each consisting of one or more applications carefully timed to the annual emergence period of the beetles

❏ larval activity continues within the wood until eradication is completed. This may present a problem with highly active attacks causing significant structural damage

❏ the smoke deposits are widely distributed and can affect other surfaces and occupants of a building; therefore the deposits must be cleaned from accessible non-wood surfaces not intended for treatment

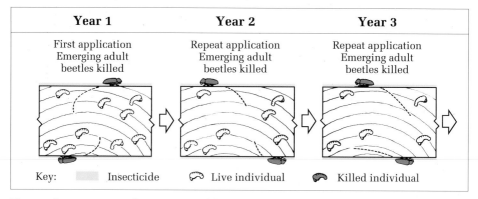

Year 1	Year 2	Year 3
First application Emerging adult beetles killed	Repeat application Emerging adult beetles killed	Repeat application Emerging adult beetles killed

Key: ▨ Insecticide 🐛 Live individual 🐛 Killed individual

How smoke treatment works against wood-boring insects

Gas fumigation

Fumigation, usually using methyl bromide gas, is an effective method of eradicating wood-boring insects if infested timbers can be enclosed temporarily in an atmosphere of the gas. The insects are killed by direct toxic action of the gas which diffuses into the damaged timber. However, the treatment provides no residual protection against reinfestation. Whole-house fumigations are carried out in some tropical countries against termite infestations but, in the UK, fumigation against wood-boring insects is normally only undertaken with moveable items, such as museum exhibits, which can be treated inside a gas-tight chamber. The extensive sealing required, and the toxic hazard associated with the fumigant gas, generally makes routine use of fumigation impracticable in buildings in the UK. Methyl bromide and similar gases can be applied only by experts using Home Office approved procedures.

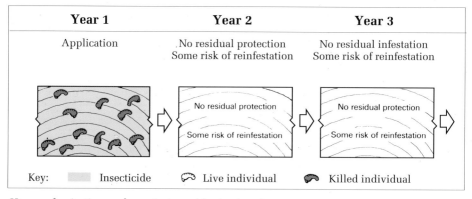

Year 1	Year 2	Year 3
Application	No residual protection Some risk of reinfestation	No residual infestation Some risk of reinfestation

Key: ▨ Insecticide 🐛 Live individual 🐛 Killed individual

How gas fumigation works against wood-boring insects

Heat sterilisation

A temperature of 52–55 °C for 30–60 minutes is lethal to all wood-boring insects found in the UK. If these conditions are maintained throughout a piece of infested wood, it will be completely sterilised. In the UK, heat sterilisation is used commercially only in the kiln-sterilisation of sawn hardwoods which have become infested with Lyctus powderpost beetle during storage. In some European countries, roof space infestations by the house longhorn beetle are sterilised by a hot-air process. The air is heated by a mobile heating unit and then introduced into the roof through ducts. This treatment method has not yet been applied in the UK.

Treatments for specific insects

Common furniture beetle

An infestation by common furniture beetle should be effectively eradicated by a single spray application of a suitable preservative product to the infested timbers. Brush application is effective but is less practicable on all but small areas.

Either a solvent or emulsion-based product is suitable. Since common furniture beetle infestations are rarely of structural significance, the slower action of the emulsion-based products is normally unimportant and is often the preferred choice due to their lower fire hazard and presenting fewer problems with residual solvent fumes. In the unusual situation where an infestation is assessed as being active and so severe as to have structural implications, the contractor should consider the use of a solvent or paste product. Clearly timbers already substantially weakened will need to be replaced or repaired.

House longhorn beetle

This insect causes relatively rapid damage, often leading to structural weakness. Effective treatment requires:

❏ thorough investigation of timbers to establish the extent of infestation and the degree of structural weakening so as to determine the need for replacement or supplementary strengthening of timbers

Timber attacked by house longhorn beetle: the surface skin of wood has been lifted to show the damage beneath

❑ application of a penetrating preservative product to all retained timbers in the roof and floor areas affected. Spray-applied solvent-based fluids or paste products are the most effective. Simple emulsion-based liquid treatments which achieve only low levels of penetration are not normally suitable

Deathwatch beetle

Infestations by this insect are normally only found in buildings more than 100 years old built with hardwood timbers such as oak or elm. Also, the infestations are usually of many years standing and associated with persistent dampness and minor decay problems with embedded timbers. Typically, an infestation will be localised in timbers such as wall plates, truss ends, bonding timbers, wall frames and panelling, where these are in contact with damp masonry. Generalised attack may also occur in buildings with dampness problems caused by condensation (eg, traditional church buildings with intermittent heating or poor ventilation). Damage may ultimately become severe and the structural consequences must be considered carefully.

Effective treatment requires:

❑ in the long term, measures to reduce the dampness and decay problems associated with the infestation. The measures for drying and localised protection of timbers from moisture are described in Chapter 6

❑ in the short term, measures to reduce insect activity in timbers which cannot readily be dried. This generally demands the application of preservative products. In small-section timbers or where infestation is limited to sapwood edges of only about 30 mm depth, solvent-based fluids, applied by spray, will provide some measure of control. Unless a preservative manufacturer can indicate effectiveness in eradicating deathwatch beetle infestation, emulsion-based products should be regarded as unsuitable due to their low

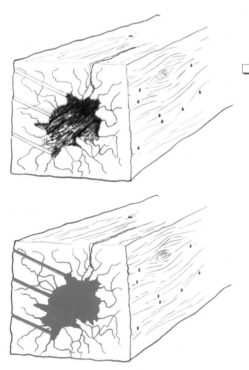

Injection of timber infested by deathwatch beetle

levels of penetration. On the larger-section timbers (usually of impermeable heartwood) with which deathwatch beetle is often associated, the deeper penetration produced by paste or by drilling and injection of solvent-based fluid is more effective. Such treatments, however, need only be applied to the areas of timbers identified as being significantly infected

Where, in large timbers, cavities are detected which are caused by a combination of decay and insects, and replacement of the timbers is not necessary, paste or solvent-based fluid should be injected. It must be noted that in persistently damp, impermeable large-section timbers, a single application of preservative is unlikely to provide complete control and repeated applications may become necessary in subsequent years. Indeed, where dampness cannot be controlled, gradual replacement of deteriorated timbers over a period of many years may be appropriate.

In cases of buildings of particular historical or architectural value, the cost of gas fumigation or heat sterilisation may be justified for major deathwatch beetle infestations. These treatments are only available from major specialist treatment contractors.

Lyctus powderpost beetle

Remedial measures against this insect are rarely necessary. Attacks can be found in:

❑ sapwood edges of hardwood timbers in older traditional buildings and therefore extinct — the insect is only able to infect timbers for up to about 10 years after felling and conversion, or

❑ modern hardwood joinery where the damage is far advanced when first noticed, and replacement rather than remedial treatment is necessary

Attacks on modern timbers are usually found on decorative timbers with clear varnish finishes; therefore treatment with conventional fluid products or pastes will be ineffective unless the finishes are first removed to allow the preservative product to penetrate. Where this can be achieved, penetrating solvent-based fluids or pastes can be expected to provide control. Simple emulsion-based products are not generally suitable since the high levels of activity associated with the insect requires a rapid-acting (ie, penetrating) product.

Since, in a modern building, infestation of timber by powderpost beetle usually starts before installation, it is normal for the building owner to seek replacement by the timber supplier rather than to attempt remedial treatment.

Table 7.3 Appropriate treatments for specific insects

	Organic solvent-based (spray or injection)	Emulsion-based (spray or injection)	Paste
Common furniture beetle	Yes	Yes, except for very large, active infestations where there is a risk of structural damage	Yes, though extra cost is rarely justified
House longhorn beetle	Yes, on lightly damaged timbers	No	Yes, on lightly damaged timbers
Deathwatch beetle	Yes, use irrigation or injection on large impermeable timbers	No	Yes, particularly on large impermeable timbers
Lyctus powderpost beetle	Yes, where sapwood is accessible	No	Yes, where sapwood is accessible, though extra cost is rarely justified

Wood-boring weevils

Specific remedial measures against weevil infestations are unnecessary as they attack only damp, decayed timbers. Removal or drying of the affected timbers provides, then, rapid eradication of the infestations.

Ptilinus beetle

Though this beetle is rarely found, any treatment required will be identical to that necessary for common furniture beetle.

Table 7.3 Appropriate treatments for specific insects *(continued)*

	Smoke	Gas fumigation	Notes
Common furniture beetle	Yes, useful DIY treatment where finances are limited (use May – August)	Yes, though extra cost is rarely justified except where infestation is widespread and access to timbers is difficult	Structural survey normally not necessary
House longhorn beetle	No	Yes, though extra cost is rarely justified except where infestation is widespread and access to timbers is difficult	Structural survey essential
Deathwatch beetle	Yes, for low but widespread attack where there is no risk of structural damage (use March – June)	Yes, though extra cost is rarely justified except where infestation is widespread and access to timbers is difficult	Structural survey essential
Lyctus powderpost beetle	No	Yes, though extra cost is rarely justified except where infestation is widespread and access to timbers is difficult	Disposal of damaged timber may be cheaper. Kiln sterilisation or gas fumigation possible for moveable items

8 The legislation controlling the application of remedial wood preservatives

In carrying out in situ remedial treatment, the specialist contractor and the operatives he employs must comply with constraints and requirements which are specified in Acts of Parliament and statutory Regulations. The more significant items of legislation and their requirements are described in this chapter. However, other legal requirements may also apply and changes resulting from European legislation are likely in the future.

Health and Safety at Work etc Act 1974

The Health and Safety at Work etc Act 1974 is a broad legislative framework applying to places of work including building sites; it is administered by the Health and Safety Executive (HSE) or by local authorities, depending on the type of building and the particular health and safety issue. The Act gives statutory status to a number of Regulations such as the Highly Flammable Liquids and Liquefied Petroleum Gases Regulations 1972, Protection of Eyes Regulations 1974, Asbestos (Licensing) Regulations 1983, and Construction (Working Places) Regulations 1966. It does the same for a number of Codes of Practice.

The main theme of the Health and Safety at Work Act is the duty on all people — employees, employers and self-employed — to take all necessary steps to ensure the safety of themselves, their employees, other workers and any other individuals whose health or safety could be at risk as a result of their work. This means that those concerned with remedial timber treatment operations must consider the potential effects of their activities, not just on themselves but also on other site workers and building occupants. When using hazardous substances such as timber preservatives, an assessment of the risks of using the preservatives, and appropriate measures to remove or limit the risks, are a statutory requirement under the Control of Substances Hazardous to Health Regulations 1988 (COSHH) (see page 85).

An important implication of the Act is that managers must ensure that measures to eliminate or minimise risks to health are taken; where managers cannot ensure elimination of these risks, they must supply appropriate protective equipment and guidance on safe procedures, and take all reasonable steps to ensure that they are used. Employees who intentionally or recklessly misuse, or fail to use, the safety equipment provided are themselves committing an offence under the Act.

In order to comply with the Act, the specialist contractor should have produced a **safety policy document**, the contents of which should be familiar to all employees, and which should set out the measures by which the managers of the contractor propose to ensure the health and safety of their employees and other people.

Control of Pesticides Regulations 1986

The Control of Pesticides Regulations 1986 (COPR) came into force on 6 October 1986 implementing Part III of the Food and Environment Protection Act 1985 (FEPA). Under these regulations, all pesticidal products (which includes wood preservatives and dry rot wall solutions) are granted approval by Ministers under advice from the Advisory Committee on Pesticides following an evaluation of the products' safety by scientific advisers in HSE. Approval is required before a product can be advertised, sold, supplied, stored or used.

Also under the regulations, HSE, which acts as the registration authority for non-agricultural pesticides (including wood preservatives), maintains a register of all approved products. From time to time HSE reviews approvals of products and approvals may be withdrawn. **It is important to ensure that, when using old stock, its approval has not been revoked.** The list of all currently approved products is published annually under the title *Pesticides 1993*[6] (and subsequent annual editions), available from Her Majesty's Stationery Office (HMSO), and updated monthly through the *Pesticides Register*[7.] In a case of doubt concerning the approval status of a product, the Pesticides Registration Section of HSE should be consulted (see next page).

Under the terms of the COPR, remedial wood preservatives and dry rot masonry fluids can be marketed for use in two categories.

❑ Amateur use: these can be bought and used by anyone

❑ Professional use: these are available only for use by trained operatives

APPROVED WOOD PRESERVATIVES AND DRY ROT MASONRY TREATMENTS: CONDITIONS OF APPROVAL

It cannot be emphasised too strongly that failure to use an approved wood preservative or dry rot masonry treatment product in accordance with the conditions of approval shown on the product label, or the more general conditions set down in the appropriate 'Consents' detailed in the Food and Environment Protection Act 1985, is not only potentially dangerous but an offence under the Control of Pesticides Regulations 1986. The sale, supply, storage, use and advertisement of a non-approved product is also an offence under the same regulations. A product which has been approved under the COPR will bear on its container label an HSE number. Products which bear no number are not approved and must not be used.

Further information concerning the registration of non-agricultural pesticidal products may be obtained from:

Pesticides Registration Section, Health and Safety Executive, Magdalen House, Stanley Precinct, Bootle, Merseyside, L20 3QZ (tel 051-951 3535)

The product label: its significance

The product label is a statement of the conditions under which approval of a product is given. Those using the product should note the meaning and significance of the different sections of the label (see next page). The layout illustrated is an example only and other layouts are permitted and used by some manufacturers. Whatever format is used, it is important that the specialist contractor appreciates that the instructions given on the label are **not just guidance but legal requirements**. The operative applying the product cannot assume safe or effective performance unless he complies in full with the label instructions.

Product name
The exact product name must be clearly stated on the label.

'Restriction of Use' phrase
The label will carry a 'restriction of use' phrase such as FOR USE ONLY AS A WOOD PRESERVATIVE. Should the product be used in any other way, it is an offence under the Control of Pesticides Regulations 1986.

TIMBER FLUID X
FOR USE ONLY AS A WOOD PRESERVATIVE

FLAMMABLE
IRRITATING TO EYES AND SKIN

DIRECTIONS FOR USE — Dilute 1 part of Timber Fluid X with 19 parts water then apply by brush at a rate of 1 litre of product per 2.5 square metres of surface.

PRECAUTIONS —
WASH SPLASHES from skin or eyes immediately.
WASH HANDS AND EXPOSED SKIN before meals and after use.
KEEP AWAY FROM FOOD, DRINK AND ANIMAL FEEDING STUFFS.
KEEP IN ORIGINAL CONTAINER, tightly closed, in a safe place.
KEEP OUT OF REACH OF CHILDREN
CONTAINS:
ACTIVE INGREDIENT A X% w/w (mg/litre)
This product is approved under The Control of Pesticides Regulations 1986for use as directed.HSE No. 0000
Use only in accordance with the directions on the label.

CONTAINS: 25 LITRES
BATCH NO. XXXX

IRRITANT

STATUTORY CONDITIONS RELATING TO USE

FOR USE ONLY AS A WOOD PRESERVATIVE.
FOR PROFESSIONAL USE.
Apply at the rate of 1 litre of product per 2.5 metres of wood surface.
The (COSHH) Control of Substances Hazardous to Health Regulations 1988 may apply to the use of this product at work.
FOR USE ONLY BY PROFESSIONAL OPERATORS.
FLAMMABLE. AVOID naked flames and hot surfaces.
Engineering control of operator exposure must be used where reasonably practicable in addition to the following items of personal protective equipment.
WEAR SUITABLE PROTECTIVE CLOTHING (COVERALLS) AND SYNTHETIC RUBBER/PVC GLOVES when using.
AVOID EXCESSIVE CONTAMINATION OF COVERALLS AND LAUNDER REGULARLY.
However, engineering controls may replace personal protective equipment if a COSHH assessment shows they provide an equal or higher standard of protection.
WHEN USING DO NOT EAT, DRINK OR SMOKE.
DO NOT APPLY TO SURFACES on which food is stored, prepared or eaten.
REMOVE OR COVER ALL FOODSTUFFS before application.
AVOID ALL CONTACT WITH PLANT LIFE.
DANGEROUS TO FISH AND OTHER AQUATIC LIFE. Do not contaminate watercourses or ground.
UNPROTECTED PERSONS AND ANIMALS SHOULD BE KEPT AWAY FROM TREATED AREAS FOR 48 HOURS OR UNTIL SURFACES ARE DRY.
THIS MATERIAL AND ITS CONTAINER must be disposed of in a safe way.
ALL BATS ARE PROTECTED UNDER THE WILDLIFE AND COUNTRYSIDE ACT 1981. BEFORE TREATING ANY STRUCTURE USED BY BATS, ENGLISH NATURE SHOULD BE CONSULTED.

READ ALL PRECAUTIONS BEFORE USE (HSE NO. 0000).

JENNINGS AND CROFT LTD
AVENUE HOUSE, THE AVENUE, NEWTOWN, BORSETSHIRE AAA AAA
Telephone: xxxxxxxxx

An example of a product label which conforms to the requirements of the Control of Pesticides Regulations 1986

Risk' phrase and hazard warning symbol
Where appropriate, the label will carry a 'risk' phrase or phrases such as FLAMMABLE or IRRITATING TO EYES AND SKIN. This is a clear and simple statement of the nature of the hazard if the product is not used in accordance with all of the information stated on the label. The risk phrase is important in the 'risk assessment' process required under the Control of Substances Hazardous to Health Regulations.

Where relevant, the risk phrase will be accompanied by an appropriate warning symbol and word such as IRRITANT. (The figure on the previous page provides an example.)

Name and concentration of each active ingredient
The chemical name and the concentration for each active ingredient in the product must be included in the label. Wood preservatives may contain one or more fungicides or insecticides, and, in some cases, both fungicides and insecticides.

Directions for use
This section of the label states the method or methods of application and contains directions on the rate at which the product is to be applied. If the product is a concentrate (identified by the word CONCENTRATE on the label) which is to be diluted before use, the rate of dilution will be clearly stated.

Precautions
The label sets out the precautions to be taken **before, during and after** use of the product and is designed to ensure the safety of the user, the public and the environment. The label also specifies whether personal protective equipment is required, and gives general advice on the procedures to be followed should the operative come into contact with the preservative through, for example, splashes on the skin, into the eyes or inhalation of the spray. In particular this section specifies protective clothing and respiratory protective equipment as necessary.

Approval phrase
Products approved after 6 October 1986 will contain the following statement on the label: 'This product is approved under the Control of Pesticides Regulations 1986, for use as directed. HSE No....'. When a product is given approval, the HSE number that is issued must be stated as part of the approvals statement.

Other information
The name and address of the company marketing the product will appear on the label, together with the size of the pack or container

which is important in assessing the quantity to be applied and the dilution rates.

Finally, it must be remembered that, as pesticides, wood preservatives are designed to kill or control the growth of certain living organisms and are potentially harmful to others. However, approved wood preservative products can be applied safely provided they are used in accordance with the information provided on the label. Therefore it is vital that the user reads, understands and complies with all the information provided on the label.

Control of Substances Hazardous to Health Regulations 1988

To comply with the Control of Substances Hazardous to Health 1988 (COSHH) Regulations, which are given statutory power by the Health and Safety at Work Act, the following procedures must be followed at any workplace (including a building site).

❑ Any hazardous material — for example, a product carrying a hazard warning such as IRRITANT, as well as materials such as dusts, mineral fibres, mould spores, etc, which could be generated during work — must be identified prior to work starting.

❑ A **written** assessment of the risk to health imposed by the identified material or materials during the proposed operations — for example, risk of breathing in dust, or risk of skin absorption of the preservative product — must be prepared.

❑ Appropriate procedures and protective equipment to reduce risks to acceptable levels (see Chapters 9 and 10) must be provided.

Where appropriate, the following procedures must also be undertaken:

❑ appropriate training of those working with all hazardous materials (including preservative products and dusts generated during preparation for treatment operations)

❑ monitoring of exposure to hazardous materials

❑ health surveillance

Further guidance on COSHH can be found in the Health and Safety Commission/Department of the Environment publication, *Remedial timber treatment in buildings: a guide to good practice and the safe use of wood preservatives*[8], and in the *Approved Code of Practice: the safe use of pesticides for non-agricultural purposes*[9].

In the case of remedial timber treatment, monitoring of exposure to hazardous materials and health surveillance are not, at present, routine procedures. Training is dealt with in more detail in Chapter 9.

Wildlife and Countryside Act 1981

As part of the initial inspection of a property which could lead to remedial treatment operations, timber surveyors and contractors should check for the presence of bats.

All bats are protected under The Wildlife and Countryside Act 1981. Where work is required on a structure that is known to be (or suspected of being) inhabited by bats, the Act requires that English Nature, the Nature Conservancy Council for Scotland, the Countryside Council for Wales, or the Northern Ireland Department of the Environment (all are successor organisations to the Nature Conservancy Council) must be consulted beforehand. Similarly, if, during treatment operations, bats are found to be present, work must stop until the appropriate nature conservation organisation has been consulted. Some wood preservatives are particularly toxic to bats. The nature conservation organisation will advise on the treatment procedures least likely to affect the health of a bat roost. Failure to comply with these requirements can result, and has resulted, in prosecution.

Legislation concerning the packaging and transport of preservative products

The operator and driver of a vehicle used for transporting timber treatment products must meet the requirements of various pieces of legislation, mainly deriving from the Health and Safety at Work etc Act 1974.

Legislation which covered the packaging and transport of chemicals (including preservative products) — the Classification, Packaging and Labelling of Dangerous Substances Regulations, also known as the 'CPL Regulations' — has been replaced by the Chemicals (Hazard Information and Packaging) Regulations 1993, known as the

A vehicle used for carrying preservative products should display prominently the appropriate hazard warning signs

'CHIP Regulations'.

However, from 1 April 1994, the part of the CHIP Regulations concerned with carriage (ie, transport) will be put into a new set of Regulations, the Carriage of Dangerous Goods by Road and Rail (Classification, Packaging and Labelling) Regulations, while the remainder of the CHIP Regulations — concerned with supply — will be updated later in the year.

Under the Road Traffic (Carriage of Dangerous Substances in Packages etc) Regulations 1992 — the 'PG Regulations' — treatment contractors must provide each of their vehicles carrying flammable chemicals with an appropriate and effective fire extinguisher; and the vehicle must bear hazard warning signs, applicable to the preservative products being carried, in prominent positions. The Road Traffic Regulations are to be reviewed later in 1994.

Relevant Approved Codes of Practice are published in *Classification and labelling of dangerous substances for carriage by road in tankers, tank containers and packages* [10] and *Packaging of dangerous substances for carriage by road* [11]. A small booklet, *The complete idiot's guide to CHIP* [12], provides a basic introduction to CHIP and is available free from HSE.

9 Preparing for safe application of wood preservatives

The aim of current pesticide legislation is towards reducing the use of pesticidal products to that which is assessed as being absolutely necessary.

A first priority, therefore, should be to apply a wood preservative product or dry rot masonry treatment only where there is an identified risk of deterioration, and then only to those areas affected and on a scale appropriate to the problem (see Chapters 6 and 7). It is important that 'dual purpose' products (ie, containing a fungicide **and** an insecticide) are not used where a 'single purpose' product would suffice.

Having identified a genuine need for the application of preservative and selected an appropriate product, and having prepared a plan which limits the scale of treatment to just that which is necessary, the next step is to ensure that the preservative product is used safely.

The primary aim of contemporary health and safety legislation is to ensure that the

The specialist contractor and his operatives need to be aware of the many people, animals and environments that must be protected against the effects of chemicals used in treatment operations

GET OUT THE FUCKING WAY!

specialist contractor takes steps to protect the health and safety of the following:

❏ the operative (ie, the person applying the preservative)

❏ others working on or visiting the site

❏ members of the public, including the occupants of the buildings being treated and their neighbours

❏ wildlife

❏ the environment

The previous chapter has already dealt with two essential elements of health and safety:

❏ the examination of the product label on the preservative container to ensure that the specialist contractor and the operative are aware of any restrictions or conditions under which approval for use under the Control of Pesticides Regulations 1986 (COPR) has been given

❏ the production of a written risk assessment and identification of appropriate protective measures as required by the Control of Substances Hazardous to Health Regulations 1988 (COSHH)

When planning the work to meet legal obligations, and before site work commences, the specialist contractor should, in addition, consider fully the other safety issues raised in this chapter and the next.

Training

It is essential that all specialist contractors and their operatives carrying out remedial treatment of timber are properly trained and competent in the work to be undertaken. This is required under Section 2 of the Health and Safety at Work etc Act 1974 and in the conditions of the general Consents relating to the storage and use of pesticides under the COPR. The minimum level of competency required is that specialist contractors must be able to recognise when the use of a wood preservative product or dry rot masonry fluid would present a risk to themselves or others, wildlife or the environment, and subsequently adopt safe procedures for the protection of these groups **before, during and after** application of the product; in particular:

❑ select the most suitable product, taking into account the hazards posed by the product (eg, flammability) and the particular circumstances of use

❑ determine the appropriate amount of the product to be used

❑ select and maintain the appropriate protective equipment and clothing

❑ identify the potential effects of exposure to the product and be able to deal with any emergency arising from the use of the product. This must include knowledge of when and how to seek specialised assistance

❑ identify and follow appropriate procedures to avoid personal contamination

❑ identify and follow safe procedures for storing, handling, decanting, mixing and disposing of products. Also carry out correct procedures for cleaning and storing personal protective equipment, clothing and other related items

❑ identify the relevant legal requirements which apply to the storage, use and disposal of products

Transporting wood preservatives

As well as meeting the requirements of the Road Traffic Regulations described in Chapter 8 as regards fire extinguishers and hazard warning signs, the specialist contractor and his drivers should adopt the following safety practices.

❑ Only the minimum amount of product required for the work to be undertaken should be transported to the site; ideally it would be organised on a daily basis. This necessitates accurate estimation of the quantities of preservative to do the work.

❑ Care must be taken during transport to prevent damage to containers; therefore drums and other containers must be secured in the van to prevent movement.

❑ Preservative products should not be transported in the same compartment as the driver and passengers where reasonably practicable. Vehicles used for transporting these products should be designed and constructed with this requirement in mind, and preferably fitted with airtight bulkheads between driver and passenger compartments and goods compartments.

❑ Containers must be labelled correctly.

❑ Appropriate and correct data about products being carried must be available in vehicles and at the contractor's office; particularly data which will enable the emergency services to deal with any incident involving actual or potential spillage or fire.

❑ When not in use, a vehicle used to transport or to provide short term storage for the products must be kept locked and supervised or in a secure compound. A vehicle should not be used for storing preservative products except in the short term (eg, at the most, sufficient supply for that day's work).

Storing wood preservatives

Poor storage and handling of products present a potential risk to operatives, other people and the environment. The storage of pesticides such as wood preservatives is covered by a variety of regulations including the Food and Environment Protection Act and local planning laws. Whenever possible, preservative products should be transported to site and used on the same day, thus avoiding the need for construction of secure storage facilities on site. If, for some reason, this is not possible, and preservatives must be stored for some days or weeks on site, then storage chests or buildings will be required.

HSE Guidance Note CS 19, *Storage of approved pesticides: guidance for farmers and other professional users* [13], offers detailed advice on the requirements of such storage facilities. This sets out rigorous requirements in relation to siting, construction materials, security and marking.

Protecting building occupants and the general public

Before work commences, the contractor should present the occupants of the premises and neighbours who may be affected by treatment operations with a written statement which includes the following points:

❏ an outline of the proposed method of treatment involved (eg, spray or brush treatment) and the areas to be treated

❏ the names of the wood preservative products and dry rot masonry fluids to be used together with details of the active ingredients

❏ the risks to occupants, the public and the environment that the treatment is likely to present (eg, temporarily increased fire risk and inhalation of preservative spray)

❏ a clear description of the precautions to be taken by the specialist contractor to protect the occupants and neighbours **before, during and after** treatment, including specifying re-entry times after the completion of treatment

This statement may be incorporated into the report that the occupants receive as a result of the initial inspection of the premises, or provided separately.

Also, before any work starts on site, the specialist contractor or his operatives, or both, are required to protect and inform other workers and members of the public who may be exposed to wood preservative products. To this end, they must:

❏ ensure that the occupants of the premises being treated, and others likely to be affected by the work, are informed **in writing** about the ventilation required following treatment, and the appropriate re-entry time to areas which have been treated; this could be included in the initial written statement to the occupants

❏ evacuate all people and pets (including fish) from rooms and voids such as roofs where preservatives will be applied. In flats and semi-detached and terraced houses, depending on the scale of the treatment work, it may be necessary to evacuate adjoining properties or seal off the treatment areas from areas not being treated. This is particularly important in properties with common roof voids. Temporary sealing may be possible using polythene sheeting and battens, but it would have to be completely effective

 # WARNING

This area has been treated with (name/s of preservative/s)

....

....

on (date) ....

Treatment completed at (time) ....

The above-named preservative products may be harmful for a short time after treatment. Therefore this area must be kept ventilated and not be reoccupied for .... hours after the above time and date.

There is also a temporary risk of fire in this area. All sources of ignition must be excluded for 48 hours.

No smoking is allowed

No naked flames

Electrical supplies must remain disconnected

No lights and heating appliances must be operated

No gas fires or cookers must be lit

In case of emergency contact:

Williams Woodworm Control Ltd
100 London Road
Queensborough

Telephone
(office hours) 0949 123456
(24-hr emergency) 0949 100100

A typical contractor's warning notice for posting around a site

❑ display conspicuously, at entry points and other appropriate places, notices warning that chemicals are to be used; and, where this involves inflammable products, prohibit smoking and naked flames in the treatment areas. These notices must be dated and timed to give a clear indication of when treatment is to be undertaken and when the occupants may return to the treated areas

❑ ensure that the treated areas are thoroughly ventilated to the open air to reduce residual fumes or vapour. Members of the public, the occupants of the building and any other people who may enter partially treated buildings should be prohibited from entering treated areas for the minimum time period stated in the conditions of use on the product label (normally 48 hours), and at least until surfaces are dry. Pets, including fish, should not be returned during this period. Any carpets which have been moved should not be replaced until the preservative used has dried

❑ before carrying out work in premises occupied by the elderly or the very young, such as a hospital or nursing home, ensure that specialist advice is sought from the medical practitioner responsible for the patients to ascertain whether the treatment will impose particular health risks. Similarly, medical advice should be sought before treatment takes place in areas occupied by people with respiratory or allergy problems. Should the introduction of preservative chemicals be considered unwise, the replacement of affected timbers may be the only course of action available

Protecting treatment operatives

Providing appropriate protective clothing

Under the COSHH Regulations, all employers are obliged to ensure that the exposure of employees to hazardous substances is prevented or controlled.

The Regulations require employers to control exposure by placing a higher priority on engineering controls than on protective equipment. The provision of adequate ventilation, and using safe working systems and safe handling procedures are examples of engineering controls.

With remedial timber treatment, it is often impracticable to provide adequate ventilation which totally removes the risks from solvent fumes and spray mists. In these circumstances, then, operatives will need to be protected by personal equipment and clothing. Small scale applications by brush usually only require gloves and coveralls. For spray application or pressure injection of wood preservatives or dry rot masonry fluids, the following items of personal protective equipment should be considered essential.

A coverall incorporating a hood
A disposable, laminated paper coverall with
elasticated wrists and ankles is adequate. In
situations where there are risks of head contact with
low beams, etc, protective helmets may be required.

Protective footwear
Such footwear should be resistant to the
products to be used, be suitable for use in wet
conditions, have slip resistant soles and conform
to BS 1870:Part 2 or Part 3. Normal types of
everyday footwear are not suitable for use when
applying wood preservative products as they
can be penetrated by some chemicals.

*Gauntlets, long gloves or alternative hand and
wrist protection*
They should be impervious to the chemicals to
be used. Those made of Viton, Neoprene,
Nitrile rubber, or 1 mm-thick PVC are
usually suitable. When in doubt, the
advice of manufacturers of the gloves
and the manufacturers of the wood

*A fully equipped
operative*

preservative should be sought. In general, unlined gloves with
separate cotton liners are better than lined gloves.

Respiratory and eye protection equipment

Where necessary, following a COSHH assessment, respiratory
equipment of an approved type must be provided and worn. (HSE
publication HS(G)53, *Respiratory protective equipment: a practical
guide for users*[14], provides more detailed guidance on selection of
appropriate equipment.)

❏ In general, the spray application of preservative products will
   require a minimum of a half-mask respirator fitted with an
   absorbent filter canister appropriate to the product being sprayed.

❏ The canister must be changed regularly. Although following the
   manufacturer's instructions is recommended, these instructions are
   not always precise. It is difficult to give specific guidance as to the
   time period: as a rule of thumb if solvent can be smelt through the
   mask, the filter in the canister is exhausted. It is good practice to
   change the canister after a maximum of one working day.

❑ Goggles or a face visor should be worn when spraying wood preservative or dry rot masonry fluid.

❑ Where injection techniques are being used, suitable splashback guards or barriers should be used to prevent any skin contact with the product.

Fire, electrical and explosion hazards

Many solvent-based preservative products are flammable and can therefore present a fire risk during application and drying. This risk will increase when the product is being applied in a confined space such as a small attic. Emulsion-based products may also be flammable in their concentrated form. Flammability hazards and other precautions are found on the product labels.

Care must be taken at all times to minimise the risk of fire. The following points should be used as a guide.

❑ Provision should be made on site for immediate access to fire extinguishers of the dry powder type. Refer to the preservative manufacturer for advice on the size of extinguishers. These must be within easy and safe reach of the operative and must be serviced and maintained for immediate and effective operation.

❑ Electrical circuits within the treatment area must be isolated before treatment starts and remain so for at least 36 hours after completion of the work. Also, cables and junction boxes must be protected against treatment fluids by the use of suitable sealants such as polythene sheet and mastic putty.

❑ It is vital that the contractor's treatment equipment, such as lighting and compressors, is correctly earthed or double insulated or operated at reduced voltages (110V CTE systems or 50V AC systems) from a mains transformer located outside the treatment area. The use of equipment with safety devices, such as earth leakage circuit breakers (ELCBs) and residual current devices (RCDs), is also highly recommended.

❑ All electrical equipment and wiring used by a timber treatment contractor must be checked monthly by a competent person. Any defective equipment must be immediately withdrawn from use and replaced.

❑ Care should be taken to ensure that all potential sources of ignition, including electric fires, cookers, open fires, and solid fuel, oil and gas heating appliances, and telephones and other electrical equipment, are switched off or extinguished and allowed to become cold prior to treatment with flammable products. These appliances should not be reused for a period of 36 hours after completion of treatment with flammable products.

❏ There must be no smoking on site at any time, and warning signs to this effect should be conspicuously displayed.

❏ If fire occurs, especially in older buildings, the contractor should always summon the fire brigade, even if the fire appears to have been successfully extinguished.

10 Safety procedures during and after treatment operations

Proper training, safe transport and storage of products, and the provision of appropriate protective equipment and clothing, as detailed in Chapter 9, will go a long way towards reducing any risks associated with treatment activities. This chapter details some additional considerations concerned with the way in which the treatment process itself is carried out, and the cleaning and reoccupation of treated areas.

Mixing and dispensing the product

When mixing and dispensing a product, the operative should avoid direct contact with the formulation. The following safety points must be remembered.

❑ Dilution of concentrates and dispensing of solutions into spray equipment should be carried out in the open air — not inside a van, in domestic premises or a similar enclosed space, or in a public place — using containers and methods which avoid splashing.

❑ The operative must read the product label and follow the dilution instructions carefully.

❑ The operative should clearly mark the containers containing the diluted product with the product name and the proportions of product concentrate and water in the dilute solution. Confusion between the diluted and undiluted product could endanger the health of the operative and others.

❑ A supply of clean water for washing should be kept near the site of dilution or dispensing. Ideally this should be in a hand basin. Eye washing facilities should also be near to hand.

❑ There should be no smoking, eating or drinking during dilution and dispensing processes.

Spillage

In the event of treatment fluid being spilled, it should be cleared up using sand or a similar absorbent material and, if necessary, by washing with detergent and water. It is important to emphasise that this waste water should not be allowed to enter any drains but disposed of safely. Refer to the relevant waste regulation authority for information and to report any major spillage. Inform the National Rivers Authority, or the relevant river purification board in Scotland, if a spillage enters a watercourse.

Safety during treatment operations

Spraying procedures

Good practice, aimed at reducing exposure of operatives to preservative products, requires that:

❑ during treatment operations, only operatives are allowed in the area or room being treated. All people not essential to the work in hand should be excluded. Animals should also be kept away from treatment areas (also see requirements for bats on page 86)

❑ each operative applies preservative products as far from his body, particularly his face, as is comfortably possible

❑ to reduce the risks of inhalation of spray mist or of drift onto non-target surfaces, only low pressure coarse sprays must be used

Access and exits

A safe working environment, and a safe means of access and exit, must be provided for all operatives. In the planning stage, prior to chemical treatment, the following points should be covered.

❑ In roof spaces and attics, fragile or loosely laid floors, and routes to and from these areas, must be covered with suitable boarding.

❑ If there is a risk of falling more than 2 m, or though fragile material, a suitable and stable working platform with guard rail and toe board must be provided.

❑ Care should be taken by operatives to avoid the need to crawl over areas already treated.

Ventilation

Where work is to be carried out in confined spaces, a safe system of work must be devised to avoid risks presented by fire or toxic fumes. Therefore the area being treated must be naturally or mechanically ventilated throughout the application period. Mechanical forced-air ventilation is rarely practical except in unusual circumstances.

Good practice requires that:

❑ rooms are treated with windows and doors open to provide adequate ventilation

❑ roof voids are treated with loft hatches open and eaves clear for ventilation; roof voids may need to be treated in sections

❑ underfloor voids treated from above with an angled lance have the floorboards lifted every 1 or 2 m to give access, and that these floorboards are not replaced after treatment to allow ventilation of fumes to the outside air — a process which usually takes 48 hours

❑ rooms adjacent to, and above and below, treatment areas should also be ventilated to avoid build up of solvent vapours permeating through from treated timbers

❑ cellars need care — all entrances must be left open and, in some instances, floorboards on the floor above will have to be lifted to increase ventilation

❑ the operative must always be aware that, **in confined spaces with limited ventilation, there is always a danger that solvent fumes can exclude oxygen thereby rendering respirators of the absorbent type useless.** Ways of increasing ventilation in confined voids must be sought or the work may have to be carried out as a series of brief sessions interspersed by lengthy periods of ventilation

❑ in those cases where mechanical ventilation is required, the ducting to any ventilation system must be made of fire-resistant metal sheet. The fan motor should be in a non-hazardous area (ideally in the open air) and out of the path of flammable vapours

❑ treatment work is started and taken through to completion in such a way that the flow of air carries any preservative spray and fumes away from the operative; this applies whether ventilation is by natural or mechanical means, but remembering that, with natural ventilation, the wind — and therefore the flow of air through a building — can change direction

Dust

Preparatory work such as the drilling of wood, cleaning, rubbing and brushing down, may lead to the release of dust and other materials, such as mould spores, into the air. These can cause respiratory problems and skin irritation. Therefore, wherever possible, a dustless method of cleaning should be used; a Type H vacuum cleaner is recommended. Dust falls within the scope of the COSHH Regulations and must be controlled as far as is reasonably practicable, and filter masks provided where airborne dust is unavoidable.

Water storage tanks and pipework

To prevent the contamination of water, water storage tanks in buildings must be tightly covered with a plastic or similar covering over which a second, absorbent covering, such as a dust cover, should be placed before work commences. Avoid spraying wood preservatives directly onto pipes and tanks since the solvent in the product may be absorbed by the plastic in drinking water pipes and tanks.

Preventing personal, water and soil contamination

It is important for operatives to remember that wood preservatives and dry rot masonry fluids can be harmful if misused. It is therefore essential for operatives to be aware of the potential health effects of accidental contamination with preservative products.

They can be absorbed into the body by:

❏ breathing in fumes or mist — treatment areas must be ventilated and respiratory protection worn

❏ skin contact — some wood preservatives and dry rot treatment products may be absorbed through the skin

❏ swallowing — this can occur if operatives who are, or who have been, using treatment products eat, drink or smoke, or put their fingers in their mouths without first washing their hands. There should be no eating, drinking or smoking on site when work is being carried out, and warning signs to this effect should be clearly displayed

Personal hygiene

Hands and other parts of the body exposed to preservatives must be washed immediately after a work shift and before eating, drinking or smoking. A bath or shower should be taken after completion of each day's work.

Personal contamination

Clean water for washing, ideally from a mains supply, should be within easy reach of the treatment area. If tap water is not locally available, buckets should be filled and brought onto the site before treatment starts. In the event of a person, clothing or equipment coming into contact with a treatment fluid:

❑ all contaminated clothing and protective equipment should be removed immediately and contaminated skin flushed with plenty of water

❑ if the eyes are contaminated, they should be washed out immediately with copious amounts of clean water (preferably tap water) for at least ten minutes

❑ contaminated clothing and protective equipment should be decontaminated immediately by washing with detergent and water

Action to be taken for anyone who appears unwell

Provided that preservatives are applied in accordance with the label instructions, they are safe and no ill effects can be expected to occur. However, all pesticides are potentially dangerous and a cautious approach should therefore be adopted towards any individual showing symptoms of ill health.

Anyone who appears unwell during or following the use of a wood preservative or dry rot masonry fluid should immediately be taken to a well ventilated place away from the treatment area and medical attention sought. If necessary, first aid measures to maintain breathing should be taken and the ambulance service called. The ambulanceman, doctor or hospital from whom medical attention is sought must be given information about the chemical that has been used — for example, the product label from the container or the manufacturer's or supplier's leaflet.

Cleaning up and reoccupying buildings after treatment operations

Reoccupying treated areas

Treated areas must not be reoccupied until the minimum time period stated in the conditions of use on the product label has elapsed — normally 48 hours or until surfaces are dry. In any event, in all areas treated with flammable products (where flammable residues and explosive atmospheric conditions can persist for some time after completion of treatment work), using gas and electric appliances, and smoking, must be strictly prohibited for 36 hours; open and enclosed fires and boilers should not be lit.

Reconnecting electricity and other services

The treated areas should be properly ventilated before electrical and gas supplies are restored. Any electrical circuits in the treatment areas which have been isolated, including those for telephones, should not be reconnected for at least 36 hours after treatment with flammable products to avoid the risk of electrical sparks in switches or appliances igniting solvent vapour.

Routine cleaning of treatment equipment and clothing

Any clothing which has been used in treatment work should be routinely decontaminated with detergent and water; these clothes must not be washed with normal domestic wear. Since the washing water must be treated as chemical waste, the contractor would be advised to consider using either disposable overalls or industrial contract cleaning services. All protective equipment, and any other equipment that has been used, should be carefully cleaned after use and stored separately from personal clothing and effects in clean, well ventilated and secure lockers. Respiratory equipment should be cleaned and disinfected before reuse. Contaminated disposable clothing should be disposed of carefully in accordance with the requirements of the local waste regulatory authority.

Disposal of unused preservative products

Products which remain unused (including concentrates, diluted solutions and empty containers), should be removed from the site and returned to a central depot for storage or for safe disposal. The waste disposal department of the local authority for the area will advise on how to dispose of surplus concentrates, solutions and containers.

Preservative products should never be left for those such as householders to use or clear up.

Under no circumstances must the run-off from a treated structure be allowed to contaminate soil, watercourses or drains. Unused products must not be poured into drains or watercourses, and must be disposed of safely.

❑ Glossary

Adult Last stage of an insect's life cycle during which it is capable of dispersal and reproduction.

Blue stain Sap stain in which discolouration is bluish.
Bore dust Excreted pellets and dust, and woody tissue fragments produced by wood-boring insects.
Brown rot Rot caused by wood-destroying fungi which digest cellulose leaving a brown friable residue of lignin.

Cellulose A major chemical component of timber.
Concentrate A solution containing a high concentration of active ingredient, to be diluted before use.
Contractor A person or firm contracting with a client to undertake inspection or treatment work. Some contractors who are individuals may do the work themselves or employ others (Operative, qv) to do it for them.
COPR Control of Pesticides Regulations 1986.
COSHH Control of Substances Hazardous to Health Regulations 1988.
CPL Regulations Classification, Packaging and Labelling of Dangerous Substances Regulations.

Damp proof course (DPC) A continuous barrier placed to prevent the passage of dampness (usually rising damp) in a wall.
Damp proof membrane (DPM) A layer or sheet of material within a floor to prevent the passage of moisture (eg, rising damp).
Decay Deterioration of timber caused by a wood-rotting fungus.
Diffusible plugs Solid plugs of water-soluble fungicide.
Dry rot A brown rot caused by the fungus *Serpula lacrymans* (formerly referred to as *Merulius lacrymans*).
Dry rot masonry treatment Introduction of a fungicide into masonry so as to hinder or prevent the growth of dry rot hyphae through the masonry.

Emergence hole Hole made by adult insect on its emergence from infested wood.
Emulsion-based (water-based) product Wood preservative product in which the active ingredients (fungicides and/or insecticides) are dissolved in one or both phases of an oil-water emulsion.

FEPA Food and Environment Protection Act 1985.
Flammable Description for any substance which readily burns.
Fruit-body Spore-bearing structure produced by fungi.
Fungal decay Decomposition of timber by fungi.
Fungi Plants characterised by saprophytic or parasitic mode of nutrition and lacking the green pigment typical of other plants.
Fungicide Any chemical used to kill fungi or to protect materials against attack by fungi.

Gas fumigation The introduction of a toxic gas into a void so as to kill pest organisms.

Hardwood Wood of trees of the botanical group Dicotyledonae.
Heartwood Inner zone of wood that, in a growing tree, has ceased to contain living cells and reserve materials.
Hypha (*pl* **hyphae**) A microscopic thread, many of which form the vegetative part (mycelium) and the reproductive part (fruit-body) of a fungus.

Infection Invasion of wood by fungi or other micro-organisms.
Infestation Establishment of wood-boring insect activity in wood.
Insecticide Any chemical used to kill insects or to protect materials against attack by insects.
Irritant Capable of causing irritation to exposed skin surfaces, eyes or respiratory tract.

Larva (*pl* **larvae**) Immature, feeding, grub-like stage of insect life cycle.
Lignin A major chemical component of timber.

Moisture content The amount of moisture, bound or free, that is present in timber; expressed as a percentage of the oven-dry mass.
Mould Superficial growth caused by non-wood rotting fungi.
Mycelium (*pl* **mycelia**) A sheet or network of microscopic threads (hyphae) of a decay fungus which grows over and through wood under attack.

Non-pressure treatment Application of a wood preservative without the use of pressure or vacuum processes; eg, by brush, dip or spray.

Operative A person carrying out the on-site remedial work, including application of preservative products. In health and safety documents, the operative is generally referred to as 'user' (of preservative products).

Organic solvent-based product Wood preservative product in which the active ingredients (fungicides and/or insecticides) are dissolved in an organic solvent, usually of the petroleum distillate type.

Paste product Wood preservative product in which the active ingredients (fungicides and/or insecticides) are dissolved in one or both phases of an oil-water emulsion which is formulated so as to form a soft paste.

Pesticide Any chemical used to kill pest organisms or to protect materials against the effects of pest organisms.

PG Regulations Road Traffic (Carriage of Dangerous Substances in Packages etc) Regulations 1992.

Pressure treatment The application of a wood preservative in which pressure or vacuum processes are used to enhance the penetration of preservative into the wood.

Pupa (*pl* **pupae**) The stage in an insect life cycle during which a larva changes into an adult.

Remedial treatment Any treatment of timber which is intended to halt or reduce the activity of existing attack by wood-destroying fungi or insects.

Respiratory protective equipment Any mask, hood, etc, which incorporates filters or absorbents intended to protect the wearer from breathing in harmful substances in the air.

Safety policy document A written statement of a contractor's safety policy.

Sapwood Outer zone of wood that, in a growing tree, contains living cells and reserve materials; generally lighter in colour than heartwood though not always clearly differentiated.

Smoke treatment The treatment of infested voids by the release of smokes consisting of finely divided particles of insecticide.

Soft rot Rot caused by cellulose-digesting micro-fungi whose hyphae penetrate the walls of wood cells; decay is normally of a superficial type.

Softwood Wood of trees of the botanical group Gymnosperms; commercial timbers of this group are confined, in practice, to the class Coniferae (conifers).

Specialist contractor A trained, professional company or individual who undertakes the inspection and remedial treatment of timber for a client.

Specifier As for Specialist contractor (qv).

Spore A microscopic air-borne reproductive body produced by a fungus.

Strand An aggregation of hyphae which has the ability to transport food and water.

Timber treatment contractor As for Specialist contractor.
Treater As for Operative (qv).

Wall sterilisation As for Dry rot masonry treatment (qv).
Wet rot Rot caused by wood-rotting fungi (other than *Serpula lacrymans*) which characteristically attack comparatively wet timber in buildings.
White rot Rot caused by wood-rotting fungi which digest both cellulose and lignin, and generally lighten the colour of wood.

❏ References

1   **Bravery A F, Berry R W, Carey J K and Cooper D E.** Recognising wood rot and insect damage in buildings. Garston, Building Research Establishment, 1992. ISBN 0 85125 535 3.

2   **Building Research Establishment.** Surveyor's checklist for rehabilitation of traditional housing. Garston, BRE, 1990. ISBN 0 85125 433 0.

3   **British Standards Institution.** Solutions of wood preservatives in organic solvents. Specification for solutions for general purpose applications, including timber that is to be painted. *British Standard* BS 5707:Part 1. London, BSI, 1979.

4   **British Standards Institution.** Wood preservation by means of copper/chromium/arsenic compositions. *British Standard* BS 4072:Part 2:1987. London, BSI, 1987.

5   **British Standards Institution.** Code of practice for the preservative treatment of structural timber. *British Standard* BS 5268:Part 5:1989. London, BSI, 1989.

6   **Ministry of Agriculture, Fisheries and Food** and **Health and Safety Executive**. Pesticides 1993. London, HMSO, 1993. (Revised annually) ISBN 0 11 242946 7.

7   **The Pesticides Register.** Ministry of Agriculture, Fisheries and Food, and Health and Safety Executive. (A monthly listing of UK approvals and other official announcements on pesticides) ISSN 0955 7458.

8   **Health and Safety Executive** and **Department of the Environment.** Remedial timber treatment in buildings: a guide to good practice and the safe use of wood preservatives. London, HSE, 1991. ISBN 0 11 885987 0.

9   **Health and Safety Commission.** The safe use of pesticides for non-agricultural purposes: approved code of practice. L9. London, HSE, 1991. ISBN 0 11 885673 1.

10   **Health and Safety Executive.** Classification and labelling of dangerous substances for carriage by road in tankers, tank containers and packages: approved code of practice. L14. London, HSE, 1993. ISBN 0 71 760629 5.

11   **Health and Safety Executive.** Packaging of dangerous substances for carriage by road. L15. London, HSE, 1993. ISBN 0 71 760628 7.

12   **Health and Safety Executive.** The complete idiot's guide to CHIP. INDG 151L. London, HSE, 1993.

13   **Health and Safety Executive.** Storage of approved pesticides: guidance for farmers and other professional users. *Guidance Note* CS 19. London, HSE, 1988. ISBN 0 11 885406 2.

14   **Health and Safety Executive.** Respiratory protective equipment: a practical guide for users. *Guidance Booklet* HS(G)53. London, HSE, 1990. ISBN 0 11 885522 0.

❏ Further reading

British Wood Preserving and Damp-proofing Association. Standards of training for operatives in safe and effective wood preservation and damp-proofing: a BWPDA guidance note. Stratford, BWPDA, 1993.

Building Research Establishment. Timbers: their natural durability and resistance to preservative treatment. *BRE Digest* 296. Garston, BRE, 1985. ISBN 0 85125 320 2.

English Nature. Bats in roofs: a guide for surveyors. Peterborough, English Nature, 1991. ISBN 1 85716 006 1.

Health and Safety Executive. In situ timber treatment using timber preservatives: health, safety and environmental precautions. *Guidance Note* GS 46. London, HSE, 1989. ISBN 0 11 885413 5.

Health and Safety Executive. COSHH and peripatetic workers. *Guidance Booklet* HS(G)77. London, HSE, 1992. ISBN 0 11 885733 9.

Health and Safety Executive. Recommendations for training users of non-agricultural pesticides. London, HSE, 1990. ISBN 0 11 885848 4.

❏ Index

A page number in bold face indicates a main section or significant item; a page number in italic indicates a reference to a figure (illustration) or photograph without a text reference on the same page.

Printed in the UK for HMSO Dd 8392699. 6/94. 287047. C30. 59226